DAD ALONE

Clavel, Phil.

Dad alone

DISCARD

Dad Alone

How to Rebuild
Your Life and Remain
an Involved
Father after
Divorce

PHIL CLAVEL

Véhicule Press

52411170

Special thanks to Tim Thomas, Linda and Paul, Viviane,
Mom and Dad, Chris and Anna, Brahm, Bill and Joyce,
Lisa, Dave, Kathy and Jean, Mary and Bob, Michelle,
Mike, Sue, Josée, Keith, Sig, Don and Carol,
Bob, Al, Alain, Raphael, and Harry.

Véhicule Press acknowledges the support of the Government
of Canada's Book Industry Development Program

Cover design: David Drummond
Inside imaging: Simon Garamond
Printing: AGMV-Marquis Inc.

Copyright © Phil Clavel 2003

CATALOGUING IN PUBLICATION DATA
Clavel, Phil
Dad alone : how to rebuild your life and remain
an involved father after divorce / Phil Clavel

ISBN 1-55065-178-1

1. Divorced fathers. 2. Father and child.
I. Title.

HQ756.C54 2003   306.874'2   C2003-903248-5

Published by Véhicule Press
P.O.B. 125, Place du Parc Station
Montréal, Québec H2X 4A3

514.844.6073   FAX 514.844.7543

www.vehiculepress.com
www.cheapthrillsguides.com

CANADIAN DISTRIBUTION
LitDistco
800-591-6250
orders @ litdistco.ca

U.S. DISTRIBUTION
Independent Publishers Group, Chicago, Illinois
800-888-4741 / www.ipgbook.com

Printed in Canada

Contents

For Meghan and Zachary

Introduction

This book does not promote divorce as a solution to marriage difficulties. It is not written with the intention of undermining the role of the mother following a divorce. It is a guide to help men fulfill their role as fathers in the aftermath of a broken marriage. I wrote this book to help dads deal with their feelings and situations, so that they may remain involved fathers following a divorce. There are concrete things that you can do as fathers that will help you maintain a close relationship with your children. Your children need you, and you have a responsibility to them. They have feelings too, of course, and they may give you mixed messages over the years. The reality is that they will always love a father who continues to provide a caring environment for them.

Becoming Aware

It has been a number of years since my wife and I separated. However, the trauma of beginning life again after seventeen years of marriage still lingers. I was always very much in control of my life and my feelings. I was the type of person people would come to with their problems, fears and anxieties. I learned that life doesn't always work out the way one plans.

The feeling that there was something wrong with my

marriage occurred in stages over a few years. It was a realization that slowly crept into my semi-conscious mind. I never spoke of this feeling with anyone. However, every once in a while I found myself looking at the "apartments for rent" column in the local newspaper. It would take a few years before I actually could admit to myself what was happening.

By the time my wife and I split up we had created two separate lives beyond the lives we shared with our children. We both had careers and were spending more time with colleagues. The two of us got together for vacations, the children's routines, and other special family events. Neither of us recognized, or would admit, what was happening. Meanwhile, the tension continued to build in the home. Something had to be done.

Little things began to aggravate us. If one person went to bed earlier than the other, it was commented on negatively. When one of us went out at night it was resented. Minor issues became major reasons to argue. Ugly words were used that had never been used before.

The Catalyst

It took a catalyst to propel me into action to deal with our marital problems. A colleague at work suffered a brain-stem stroke at the age of forty. The night of his attack I drove to the hospital to see him. I was directed to the intensive care unit. In this dimly-lit room, I stared in shock when I realized this vibrant man could now only move his eyelids. Little did I know that the unhappiness I was feeling was no longer going to remain dormant. Just as his body had trapped his spirit, seeing him had managed to free mine.

In talking to people after my marriage broke up, I learned that often a catalyst will force you to look at your life and particularly the state of your marriage. It could be another woman, or a change of workplace, or something else that will provide the incentive to act when a marriage is no longer satisfying for whatever the reason.

My Role as Dad

At the time, my son was seven and my daughter was ten years old. My children and I were very close. As parents, my wife and I had always managed to divide equally our parental duties. In addition to the regular routine, I also coached baseball and hockey, but we took turns taking the children to their swimming and ballet lessons. We took family vacations together every year. Because I am a teacher, my schedule allowed me to spend more time with the children. Most of their friends knew me well, as I was one of the few dads on the street who arrived home early each night. Household chores were also divided evenly between my wife and me. However, my wife did tend to cook most of the meals.

I'm describing my role as a father to give you a clearer picture of our lives at that time. I reviewed these roles prior to the separation. I spent endless hours attempting to assess how traumatic my departure from the home would be on the children. I reflected on my own father and wondered how my life would be different had he not been a part of my life. These thoughts caused great concern and worry. Eventually, I acknowledged that the marriage was not salvageable. However, I also came to the conclusion that my children needed me, as their father, to maintain my role as an active part of their lives.

Reflection

As a teacher I worked with many families and students who had gone through divorce. My experience showed me that children who adjusted well to a divorce seemed to have fathers who remained involved with them. I am fully aware that a divorce is extremely difficult for children of any age. However, my experience demonstrated there is greater hope for children to live happy productive lives when their dads continue to play an active part in their everyday upbringing.

Think of Their Mother

Another factor that I had to consider would be the emotional state of their mother following the collapse of a seventeen-year marriage. As a father, living outside the house, I would have to trust her to give the children the emotional support they needed at this time and in the future. The children would need to get positive messages about each of their parents from both of us. I came to the conclusion that I could depend on their mother to give them the right messages. Emotions run high during and after a divorce and sometimes little things become major challenges. This happens particularly when there are children involved. You end up:

> ▷arguing over nothing,
> ▷getting very little sleep each night,
> ▷spending more and more time out of the house,
> ▷not looking forward to going home.

There were intense discussions. We tried to keep them as discreet as possible, but the children were affected by the underlying tension.

I remember my wife yelling at me for something meaningless. No sooner did the words come out of her mouth than my daughter was repeating something similar to me. This scene played out in slow motion for me at the time, and it made one thing perfectly clear. I did not want my daughter to grow up believing that this was how married couples interact together. I realized that something had to be done quickly.

The Emotional Drain

I analyzed the situation as clearly as I could. However, I was unprepared for the emotional drain the separation would cause prior to my leaving the home. As young boys, many of us are taught to be emotionally strong. Crying is considered a sign of weakness. I could not recall ever seeing my father cry. I had seldom cried growing up. During the time of the separation, I cried more often than I had cried in my whole life. I would keep this private. I tended to cry in the shower when wondering whether I was going to lose my children. Guilt was creeping into my thoughts. Would my children ever forgive me for leaving? Would I still have access to my children? These and other questions raced through my mind.

Reaching Out

I began to share my concerns about the marriage and children with a few close friends. I was very fortunate because these friends didn't judge or comment inappropriately. Instead, they steered me in the direction of a counselor. I just took the phone number and for a long time I did not call. I still believed I could deal with the situation alone. I was wrong!

1. Getting Help

Sooner or later a third party will be needed to help you deal with the emotional as well as the pragmatic side of a separation. You may feel that you can handle everything yourself, but you will do yourself, and your children, a big favor by seeking help. Circumstances surrounding a separation can be overwhelming even for the strongest individual.

A counselor can help you grieve, deal with guilt and frustration, and prepare for dealing with your children as a single parent. I chose to see a counselor on my own only when I concluded that my marriage was not going to get better. You certainly should take every opportunity to seek counseling with your spouse if you feel that the marriage can be saved. However, it is important that both parties have this feeling.

I saw my counselor for four or five months while my separation was legalized. I worried that I was not sufficiently upset about the failure of a seventeen-year marriage. After a number of sessions, he pointed out that I had indeed been grieving for the last two years.

A counselor can help you recognize guilt and encourage you to deal with it. You may feel guilty that you are divorced or getting divorced. It could be that you have guilt because of what you feel you have done to your children. Divorce is often perceived as a sign of failure, and it certainly could weigh some people down for a long time.

My counselor helped me realize that failure is okay as long as you can pick yourself up and learn from it. Wanting to be there for my children, let alone get on with my own life, gave me lots of incentive. Let's face it: if we as fathers are going to be able to provide our children with a stable environment in our new home, we have to be emotionally stable ourselves. How can we be sensitive to our children's needs if we are constantly worried about our own?

The counselor pointed out that not everyone shows frustration, hurt, and anger in the same way. I remember remarking that my spouse was upset because she did not feel I was angry enough. I had been puzzled by this, and wondered if this was true. My counselor reminded me that people exhibit their hurt and frustration in a variety of ways. The obvious would be by yelling or crying. However, he pointed out that seeking help in an attempt to dissolve a marriage was in itself quite demonstrative of someone who is hurt and angry. This helped me understand what I was feeling.

I realized that I was dealing with this breakup in a manner that was consistent with my own personality. However, I was always conscious of the fact that I wanted the transition to be as painless as possible for my children. I was very much aware of how important it would be for them not to witness their mother and father openly fighting.

I did not want this unhappy situation to go on for longer than it already had. Emotionally, it was taking its toll on all four of us. I was a bundle of nerves, my wife was in a similar state, and the kids were becoming increasingly anxious. The children could sense the unease in the house and sought reassurance that everything was okay. This would only make the inevitable more difficult to deal with later.

The guilt over the separation continued to increase with every day that I stayed in the home, yet at the same time, the counselor was able to reassure me that a divorce, and the responsibility for it, is shared by two people. He encouraged me to remember that even though I was self–assured in many areas and felt I could deal with most things, it would be important to share the blame for the failed marriage. Once I had accepted the fact that I was not solely responsible, I would be in a better position to begin a new life and continue to be a supportive father.

I knew that my children would need me when the separation was finalized. I would not be able to be with them each day once this step was taken. I knew that children particularly suffer immediately following the separation. It would be more important than ever for me to remain an integral part of their lives. The counselor helped to prepare me for my new role as a divorced dad. I did not get all my answers from him, but those that I did get helped me to find my feet again.

Any father should be prepared to seek help so as to be better equipped to help your children in the difficult years ahead. At the very least the counselor can act as a sounding board with an objective ear. He provided a direction for practical steps that I would have to take. I was able to become more fully aware of my fragile emotional state, with its sadness, anger, and grieving for this loss. No matter how difficult or smooth your divorce is, seeing a counselor is a big step towards becoming a healthier and happier divorced dad. If you don't feel you need the help then think of it as a means of getting help for your children. It could be the best investment you make in their future happiness.

2. How Do You Tell the Children?

The most difficult thing I have ever had to do is tell my children that their mother and I were separating. I knew that this would be a moment that they would remember for the rest of their lives. One of the best ways to handle this traumatic situation is to work out a time and place where you and their mother can make the announcement together.

This is a sad and very emotional event, so if at all possible try and break the news to them as a couple. At the very least it can serve as a way to demonstrate to your children that you and their mother are still able to get together to make decisions that concern them. After all, other family crises are going to occur in the future, so it is a good time to begin cooperating with their mother on how best to deal with them.

I'm sure my children were feeling quite anxious. As I said, they could sense the tension in the home. Their mother and I felt that it was extremely important for both of us to put aside our differences and face the children together so we could gauge their reactions. In the months ahead, when their mother and I were attempting to do damage control, it helped that we had established this pattern of being able to work together.

Timing

We decided to tell the children prior to my officially leaving the home. The papers had all been signed and would be in effect in about twenty-four hours. Prior to this we had attempted to keep up the appearance of a happy couple, but I knew my daughter, who was eleven at the time, had probably not been fooled.

When the children came into the room that morning, we sat up in bed with them, held them, and told them that we were getting a divorce. Within no time, we were all in tears. My son ran off to his room while my daughter held on to her mother and me. I went after my son to try and console him, but eventually gave him the space he needed.

Allow Time for Grieving

I realized that the children would need their time to grieve. I had already had the benefit of at least two years of grieving without fully realizing it, yet I was still extremely upset! Their mother and I realized that we would have to both be there for their emotional needs even though we would be doing it in separate homes. The months that followed would be an emotional roller coaster for all of us.

It is important for a divorced dad to review this critical time in the divorce process. How did you deal with this as a family? Did you deal with it at all? Is there some repair work needed there? Are there issues that still linger? Can you and the children resolve some of these issues or do you need outside intervention? Schools, social service agencies, psychologists and, depending on the severity, hospitals, are experienced and usually equipped to deal with children and divorce issues. There may be a divorce group for dads that meets regularly near your home. You don't have to deal with all the issues alone. Sometimes an outsider can point you in a direction you had not considered.

Maintain Lines of Communication
In order to maintain a sense of how well your children are functioning following the announcement, you will have to test your own ability to communicate. I must admit that I found this very difficult. Emotionally, I felt quite fragile and was not anxious to call their mother and risk another argument. I spent many hours observing their play, checking with their friends' parents, and monitoring their progress at school. I was very fortunate that, for the most part, they continued to function as happy young children should at their age. However, I knew that they were probably hurting on the inside and sooner or later that hurt would have to come out.

I'm sure I made my share of mistakes. However, there are fundamental things that any father can do to make sure his children are emotionally secure at this time:

▷If possible, keep in contact with their mother.
▷Try not to lay blame but to focus on problem-solving.
▷Refer to friends and family who have access to the children.
▷Trust your own instincts as a father.
▷Talk to your children.
▷Learn to be a better listener.

You should know your children better than anyone else, so your instincts are probably correct. You can't allow avoidance or guilt to determine your course of action. It is important to remember your role as their father and to make decisions that will help them. You cannot hide your head in the sand when you see a problem. You cannot make decisions concerning the children based on feelings of guilt because of the failed marriage. Avoidance and guilt will only compound the problem and make life more difficult for you and the children.

3. Custody and Child Support

Custody and child support usually become the most contentious issues in any divorce involving children. Generally, the legal system tends to support mothers in this area. I would advise any father to become familiar with the divorce and custody laws in their jurisdiction. A lot of information on this subject is available on the Internet to help fathers. Information from a lawyer can also be valuable. Your objective is to understand the legal system with regard to divorce and your rights and responsibilities as a father.

I was not made fully aware of all the legalities of custody. I neglected to ask the lawyer to explain the legal difference between sole custody and joint custody. I believed at the time that joint custody meant that the children would have to live at their mother's house fifty percent of the time and at my house the other fifty percent. My wife and I both felt that this would be traumatic for the children at that time. I also felt that my wife would be extremely saddened by this arrangement.

I was attempting to make the transition as smooth as possible. Their mother had to be in a healthy emotional state as well if any healing was to take place for the children. As a result, I agreed to let their mother have sole custody with the unwritten agreement that I would have unlimited access to the children. I have been fortunate that this arrangement has not been a problem at all.

I have since learned that the civil code where I live overrules custody agreements in both health and education. It ensures, although many fathers as well as mothers may not be aware of it, that regardless of who has custody, both parents have equal say and responsibility in these two areas.

Demonstrate a Level of Respect

No matter how high the anxieties get during the emotional and legal process of separation, your children will always look for signs that there still remains a level of respect between their father and mother. They will continue to look for those signs in the months and years following the divorce. A child will wish for it and will need to see it because he/she loves both of you. Tension that lingers will increase anxiety in your children.

Respect can be demonstrated through small gestures. Most of these occur, of course, once you have finally separated officially. For instance, rather than argue over nothing, demonstrate respect for your former spouse by behaving with courtesy during your dealings with her in front of the children. This can be accomplished by discussing something non-controversial in a polite and friendly manner. At some point you may be strong enough to send her something for Mother's Day to show the appreciation you have for the role she plays as the mother of your children. I always brought a plant over for Mother's Day. (If the gesture is not sincere you may get the plant thrown right back at you.) A hug or a special greeting on a birthday or holiday will also get your children's attention.

These gestures can promote healing for your children. For me, these moves were at times difficult, yet at other times heartfelt. This practice helped me to heal. More important, it showed the children that their mother and I were okay with each other. We could come together if needed. This would be helpful because there are times, and there will be for any father, when the children force you to come together.

Remember Rights and Obligations
It is important to be extremely aware of both your rights and obligations. As angry or as hurt as you might be, you must remain level–headed enough to consider what is reasonable for both you and your children. You cannot ignore their mother. You will need to work with her to make sure your children have their needs met in the coming years. The negotiations between you and her are going to be crucial to how you communicate with each other in the future. Both parties have to leave the separation and divorce process feeling a degree of comfort or else future dis-cussions surrounding the children's issues will be jeopardized.

The legal process in a divorce can be long, unhealthy, and unfair. My former wife and I worked out custody, child support, and division of property together. Some of these things were easily negotiated while others were more contentious. The whole process took well over a year from the time we decided to separate. I'm sure there are things that we both would do differently, however, I believe we were able to make this work because we maintained a level of mutual respect.

Without that respect, it comes down to who can "beat" the other partner the most. This aggressive stance does nothing for either partner, nor does it help the emotional wellbeing of the children. That type of battle only allows either or both of the partners to use the children as pawns in a self-serving exercise.

One lawyer I had retained stated that, "I would prefer if you and your wife were fighting. I really don't like it when couples work things out together." Unfortunately, this type of statement is representative of the whole divorce process. In many places it remains a confrontational process for the two adults and, as a consequence, the children are forced to ride on an emotional roller coaster. You have to look for means to reduce confrontation.

Mediators can help. They are available in many places. Some are lawyers. Mediators can help both parties see things from a much more objective point of view. Where one party may be unreasonable, the mediator can be helpful in giving direction. Because of their experience, they can sometimes point things out that are not so obvious to the couple whose emotional stability is somewhat fragile.

Today many couples are trying to come to mutual agreements without third parties involved. This is helpful in keeping communication lines open and cuts down on legal fees. It also gives each party an opportunity to identify what is important to them in order to move on with life. Reaching an agreement remains the goal; it can be difficult to achieve.

Dealing with the Legal Process

Something that fathers would be wise to remember is that most of us don't have enough personal wealth to withstand a long court battle. The majority have a monthly income and any property and investments that the couple has managed to accrue over the years together. These can be divided, and you may lose substantial income and personal property. A long court battle will only help to deplete any of the assets that you have managed to gain over the years.

However, no judicial system has a right to keep you from your children if you are attempting to be the best possible dad. It is our right as fathers to be directly involved in our children's lives. If you have everyone's interest in mind there is no reason why you should not be an integral part of your children's lives. If the courts rule otherwise then by all means fight for your rights as a father.

Material wealth is meaningless if we are denied access to our children's daily lives. The guidance and modeling of a healthy and caring father cannot be compensated for, or replaced by, child support payments. A child's happiness and well–being are dependent on the care and support given by both parents. This is definitely a battle worth fighting.

It does not work for a father to give up everything he owns. You have a right to happiness too! You have a right to live a healthy and productive life as a father. Being divorced should not mean that your life now consists of a one-room basement apartment. You can't be healthy and productive if you do not have enough money to live each week.

The legal system is doing much more harm than good for children when it forces fathers to make child–support payments that are disproportionate to their incomes. Fathers who can't afford to be a part of their child's life because of legal judgments are being robbed of both that right and their own personal dignity as a parent. This is a battle that the individual divorced father as well as divorced fathers' groups everywhere must continue to fight. And this work needs to be done at the same time as you fulfill your children's need for a happy, supportive father who will always be there for them as a positive role model, no matter where they live.

Regardless of how the custody and child support issues are settled, the process will leave scars on each member of the family. Healing can be a slow process, but with patience and a thread of respect left between individuals, healing can begin. Over the months and years that follow, some of these wounds will reopen. There may also be periods when the relationship between the divorced couple deteriorates.

Parenting Together through the Storm

The success that parents will have with their children will be a reflection of their own happiness and sincerity. A father, whether divorced or not, is dependent on the mother's interactions with the children. A divorced father must hope and work at making sure that his children are getting consistent and fair messages from their mother about his role as their father. This is particularly important if the children are spending the majority of their time in their mother's home.

If it is determined that the children are getting mixed messages, it is important to address these issues with their mother. A father must assert his rights as a father while at the same time demonstrating consistent parenting in as calm a manner as possible. Maintaining a positive approach to problem-solving is essential if one wishes to find solutions. This will allow you to remain a positive role model and an involved caring father who is sincere. These are qualities that will allow any divorced father to maintain his place in the hearts and minds of his children.

The issues of custody and child support can be discussed forever. Divorced fathers have many stories, and all our situations are different. Whether an individual has a small income or a large one, the issues are important. While keeping fairness in mind, the bottom line is that a father needs to maintain a standard of living that will allow him to make a difference in his children's lives during the years that follow. A father cannot do that if he is emotionally distraught over having to declare bankruptcy.

A father needs to have access to his children. For him to be denied access for income–related reasons effectively provides children with a handicap that they will carry for the rest of their lives. Custody arrangements must respect both roles and the impact that both parents have on their children.

The children will need as much emotional support as possible, particularly in the months following the separation. Part of a father's emotional stability will be directly connected to his ability to remain a provider for his children. Following a separation, basic needs such as food, clothing, and shelter can loom very large for many men. These fundamentals will have to be attainable if a father is going to have an equal opportunity to continue to be a guiding force in the lives of his children. Court rulings that deprive fathers of basic needs through unreasonable child support rulings are depriving children of a healthy upbringing. Fathers who are able to rebuild their lives and maintain a close relationship with their children will make a huge difference in their lives.

The legal conclusion to a divorce will ultimately define a father's financial capabilities as well as his access to the children. However, what it cannot do is predetermine that someone will be a good divorced father. While I was married I had to work at being a good father and now that I am divorced I have to work even harder at it. It is different from the joint parenting role I had before, but just as fulfilling.

Dad First!

As a divorced dad I found myself in charge of everything which had once been shared. Reacting to your child's tantrums is totally in your hands. You no longer have that partner to help you clarify solutions and consequences as problems develop with your children. Your children will be wondering and possibly testing to see how well you cope on your own. In addition, you will have all the cooking, washing, and cleaning to do in the home.

Another important thing to remember is that you are a father first and a bachelor second. Don't get carried away with your newly-established freedom. Remember, you are trying to build a life that is best suited for your children. Many of the early decisions I made following the separation made a significant difference in the quality of our lives together. And the biggest decision you will have to make will be where you are going to live.

4. Finding a Place to Live

Your choice of residence following the separation will be extremely important. Is it close to their mother's neighborhood? Is it safe? Do the children have a bedroom? Can they bring friends over? These and many other questions will arise with your choice of apartment or house. Ideally, you want to be as close as possible to their mother's house, so it will allow them to have more access to you. This is also a big advantage for you in that it allows them to remain close to the neighborhood where their friends live. Familiarity with the neighborhood will mean less anxiety for them, and, believe me, you must be prepared for anxiety.

Having a home that is in close proximity to their mother's will allow you to be a familiar part of their daily routine. You may no longer be able to put them to bed each night, but you may be able to drive them to school on occasion. Maybe you can pick them up from their swimming, ballet, or basketball practice. I was fortunate to be able to drive my children home from school if required.

Check the Neighborhood

Far too often I've heard of fathers who moved to apartments only to discover that they are not situated in the most ideal neighborhoods for their children. Ask yourself whether you and your children will feel safe there.

Do you see any evidence of gang membership near the apartment? Are the police often at the apartment or patrolling the street where it is located? You don't want your children hanging out with kids who are constantly getting into trouble. They are at a vulnerable time in their lives. It is best not to expose them to elements that will only compound your difficulties.

Try to find a place that is quiet with neighbors who are relatively friendly. I found an apartment on a quiet residential street that was only a five-minute drive from the children's mother's house. It was divided equally between people my age and senior citizens. If you do a little homework on location, your life may be a little easier for many years to come.

Make Room for the Children

One of the most important things that my counselor discussed with me was the search for my new place of residence. I had not done anything concrete about finding a place. I was too concerned about dissolving the marriage in as compatible a manner as possible. The counselor mentioned that one of the biggest mistakes that many divorced fathers make is that they don't rent an apartment with at least one extra bedroom for the children. This never allows the children to develop a feeling of home in their father's place. He explained that many children feel secondary in their father's life when they realize there is no place for them in his new apartment. They begin to feel like an intrusion or inconvenience because every time they come over, Dad has to move out of his bed and onto the couch.

Think of your children carefully when looking for the apartment. When you are together, how well will you all function in your new space?

As you might imagine, as a result of the counselors' advice, I began to look. My two children would have to share a bedroom. I had to be realistic about my financial situation. I simply could not afford to rent a three-bedroom apartment in the ideal location. The criteria can be summed up as follows: find a place close to their neighborhood; secondly, it should be on an acceptable street; and finally, the children should be able to sleep in a room separate from their father's.

Dad's Needs Too!
Obviously, a father shouldn't ignore his own needs. Your new home will also be representative of your new life, so you want to be comfortable too. We are better fathers if we are able to find happiness again. Since I had never lived in an apartment, I knew it was going to be quite an adjustment. My personal criteria for the new place were that it should have an open-concept layout and a fairly nice view. Basically, I wanted to enjoy the feeling of coming home at the end of a working day. I knew that finances would be limited and that there would be little left over for going out at night.

Bring a Friend
When looking for your apartment or house, bring a friend to help with the assessment. Four eyes are better than two. Your friend may see things that do not immediately occur

to you. I did this when I went apartment hunting, and it made a big difference. I had someone with whom to discuss the positives and negatives of each apartment we viewed.

When I saw what I thought was an acceptable place, I received the encouragement I needed to go and sign the lease. This was a difficult thing for me to do as it was definitely closing the door on the marriage. At this point I was still at home with the children. Their mother and I had worked out the details of the separation, but this was one of the first concrete steps I had actually taken to begin life as a divorced father.

Since I had been married for seventeen years, these events seemed to be unfolding quite rapidly. Although nervous about the prospect of life alone, I felt that I had made an important step in moving ahead.

I wasn't sure whether I could afford the $600 rent, but it was close to what I was looking for. The dining and living areas were open to each other, and it had a panoramic view of the lake. Another bonus was that it was a concrete building which made it safer in case of fire, cheaper on insurance, and much more soundproof than wooden buildings. It turned out to be a choice that would keep the children and me relatively happy for three years.

To conclude, as far as finding a place to live is concerned, it is important to:

▷ Keep both your own and the children's needs in mind.
▷ Bring a friend or relative to help you.
▷ Find a place close to where the children live.

▷Make sure it is on a safe street.

This is one of the first big decisions you will have to make as a divorced father. It will make all the difference in the world to you and your children, if you put in the effort required to make the correct choice. In order for you to maintain your role as a supporting father it is important for you and your children to have a comfortable home that will allow your relationship to continue to grow.

Watch Your Budget

Following the separation, your financial resources may be somewhat restricted. Your monthly income may not allow you to live in an apartment or home in a style to which you were accustomed. You will have to depend on other resources to find the place that will be suitable for you and the children. Speak to friends, look in the newspapers, and drive around your neighborhood. You never know what you may see or hear about by letting it be known that you are in the market for a place to live. If you can avoid it, don't rush into anything too quickly.

5. Moving out of the Home

It is extremely important that your children know exactly when you are moving out. This is much better than having them wake up one day to find you gone. The feeling of abandonment can be quite frightening. It is devastating for everyone. They have a right to know what is going on and when it is going to happen. A father is a pillar in a child's life and should remain so. They need to know that you will always be there for them. This is an important time to try to get that message across to them.

By involving them in the process, without forcing them to make unreasonable decisions, you and their mother are demonstrating that you are acting in a sensible and stable manner. This is not an impulsive act as a result of a reaction to a particular incident. It also demonstrates to them your ability to cope with the stressful situation. Are you in control of your emotions? Children want to see their fathers in the best possible light and this is the worst of all situations. At this particular moment in time you only have one chance to demonstrate your qualities as a father. It is important to make the most of it.

Home Furnishings
When dividing up home furnishings, consider carefully the items that you are going to take with you. This is often a

very stressful negotiation, and you may need a third party. This is not something you want to involve the children with nor should they hear any of the discussion. Their mother and I decided to settle this as quietly as possible between the two of us. Often these discussions created more anxiety, and over trivial items. In the end, I didn't feel comfortable taking many things. I wanted the children to have the same items in the home that they had prior to me leaving. This was done despite the fact that the law where I live states that property is to be divided equally.

Some Fundamentals

If you are in the middle of separating or have just separated, there are some basic things that you will need in your new place. Unfortunately, I didn't take any of these things, so it got quite expensive to get re-equipped. Any towels you can bring with you will help you with your bathroom budget. Spare plates, pots, and knives and forks can all help reduce immediate expenses. You want to avoid putting you and the children at financial risk, so anything you can accumulate to begin your new life will help. Bedding is another expense that you will want to keep to a minimum. A friend gave me a comforter and that was a big help. Things don't have to be exactly what you want as long as they work and save you money initially.

You need much of this household equipment before the children come over to the apartment. It is going to be new and possibly frightening for them initially, so you'll want to have essentials such as these already in place. You will have to hustle to get all this together, but you want everyone to be as comfortable as possible.

The decision to leave most of the furnishings at their mother's home benefited my children because the home they grew up in would remain intact. The difficulty with the decision was that I had put myself at a tremendous disadvantage in terms of getting my apartment to function like a home. I had no idea of the challenge that lay ahead for me. I suppose it was naïve to think that I could get the apartment to look like a home for the three of us. I had been working for nineteen years, yet when I left I took little more than my clothes.

The Day of the Move

When the day finally came to move out of the house, their mother and I had arranged for her and the children to go on a short trip. We didn't want them to have a lasting image of their father packing his belongings and leaving their home. The other thing we wanted to avoid was a last minute argument over something trivial. I arranged for a friend to help me. I borrowed a van, moved some personal items, a few furnishings, and the task was completed in one morning. Having a friend was a great help both for the labor and the emotional support.

Leaving the children's home is a delicate operation. Remaining calm and supportive in an emotionally charged situation is not always easy. Easing the children's separation anxiety is an important part of the process. You can do this by reassuring them that you love them, through hugs and words of comfort. Here are some other reminders:

▷ Remind them that you will not be far away.

▷ If you know where you are going to move, bring them to have a look at the outside of the place.

▷ Let them know when you will be leaving and avoid having them be there when you are packing.

▷ Don't forget to leave them a phone number where they can reach you!

▷ Leave the house in good order for when they return.

▷ Write them each a note and put it in their bedrooms.

6. The Transition and Your Support System

The apartment was not ready when I moved out, but this turned out to be a blessing in disguise. I moved all of the items to my sister's and stored them in her garage. She had offered to allow me to stay in her home until the apartment was ready. I would end up living there for a few weeks. I did not realize how important this time at my sister's house was going to be for my emotional well–being.

Slowly, it began to occur to me that I had never lived alone. I had moved from my parent's house into a duplex with my new wife as smoothly as a Formula One driver shifts gears. I began to wonder whether I could cope on my own. Self-doubt began to creep into my thoughts. What would it be like to come home at the end of the day and have no one to talk to each night? My children wouldn't be there to have dinner with and tuck into bed. Would I be able to maintain a home on my own and care for the children when they came over? Would we ever to be able to have fun again?

Relatives and Friends

The time at my sister's house was an important transition. I would recommend this intermediate step to anyone in a similar situation. My sister and brother-in-law were both great listeners as well as caregivers. They provided a calm home environment for me that was what I needed, given the turmoil I had been living for the last few months. It was comforting to know that someone cared for me. I was a bundle of nerves and tremendously unsure of what lay ahead.

Sharing

By opening up with people and sharing anxieties and fears, I was able to find support for what I was going through. Many people have either gone through a similar experience or know of someone who has. They are sometimes able to help shed light on something that may not be so obvious to someone who is in the middle of the storm. Relatives who you may not have been that close with in the past can be supportive and rally to your side. Remember: fathers have a need to feel comforted and supported too.

My sister and brother-in-law were two of the first people I discussed the anxiety of the separation with in more detail. Each night at dinner, I would have the opportunity to share a feeling or detail of something that had occurred. In certain instances they would offer practical suggestions, but they always allowed me to use my judgment as to how I wanted to proceed.

Choose Carefully

A divorced father has to decide whom he wants to turn to for support. A father shouldn't be obliged to share his divorce experience with anyone, especially at this critical period. Some people are just too opinionated and will only make you feel more uncomfortable than before. I learned, quickly, that there are people that don't believe in divorce no matter what. These people can only serve to frustrate someone who is going through such a difficult period in their life. My experience has shown me that people like that cannot understand that it may be necessary for two people to part in order that they be able to move on with their lives. You can waste valuable time and energy attempting to make these people understand your plight.

Avoid Debates

During the period immediately after leaving the home, I was not interested in ideological debate regarding the merits of marriage and divorce. I kept my distance from people who were. My moods varied, but I was in control enough to realize that I needed people who would help bring me back to that level of health and happiness that I once knew. A divorced father will have many emotional valleys in the years following a divorce. It is important that he surround himself with friends and family who will help get him through those low periods.

No matter how the final divorce settlement reads, there will always be people who will feel obligated to give you their opinion on it, with comments such as "Why are you paying child support?" "How come you didn't get half the furniture?" "You should have the kids all the time!" A good comeback is to state that the settlement was in the best interest of everyone at the time. You may want to make adjustments as time goes by, but this is not the time for second-guessing.

Dealing with Reality

I believed in myself enough to know that I would work my hardest to pick myself up and get my life back on track. The only problem was that I had not thought out the practical obstacles that would be in my way. Furniture and enough money to live on were two concerns that immediately came to mind. I was so worried about my children's emotional state as well as a peaceful resolution to the separation that I ended up in need myself. I had ignored the realities of everyday life that would be awaiting me when I moved out of my sister's home.

I recommend a transitional living accommodation for any divorced father who has some reliable friends or relatives. This transition can be pivotal in shifting your attention from what has transpired to what is yet to come.

▷The transitional period can be a healthy exercise for any divorced father. It can allow for time to reflect on what has transpired.

▷A caring environment can do a lot for emotional healing in a short period of time.

▷It allows time to consider the realities of life as well as time to begin careful planning for those realities.

7. Staying Focused at Work

One thing that helps a divorced father take care of his children's needs is to make sure he is doing the right things at work. This is a volatile time, yet it is more important than ever to be productive so as to be able to provide for yourself and your children. The periods prior to and just following the separation are extremely difficult times. I knew that my ability to concentrate on tasks at work had diminished. I was aware of the difference in my performance. Since I was getting little sleep at night, I found my nerves were quite raw.

Speak to Your Supervisor
One of the best things a divorced dad can do is to let his superior know he is having marital difficulties. I decided to let my superior know that I was having problems during the time leading up to the separation. He was quite sympathetic. He told me that he had not noticed any deterioration in my work and that I could take all the time I needed to deal with it. Another administrator told me that under similar circumstances, he did not feel he would be able to cope at work. Needless to say these comments were reassuring to me in terms of their vote of confidence for my job performance.

Colleagues Can Help

Colleagues were also quite helpful when I decided to share with them some of what I was going through. Some of my closest colleagues were able to support me on a daily basis in terms of work as well as personal issues. It was helpful that some of them knew my children and were experienced parents themselves. They were extremely helpful in giving sound advice, particularly when it came to emotional issues involving the children. Another perspective goes a long way when you are so frustrated that it is difficult to think.

It has been over six years since the separation and I no longer carry that emotional baggage into my workplace every day. However, some of those same people are still there and are always willing to offer sound advice. It's good to know that you have faithful people around you who care about your welfare. If a divorced dad can find parents in the workplace who can offer sound objective advice, this will be extremely helpful. As a single parent, it is sometimes wiser to bounce ideas off of others before taking action.

In conclusion, here is some advice for fathers who want to bring up issues at the workplace:

▷ Consider informing your superiors.
▷ Don't spend endless hours discussing your personal problems at work.
▷ Seek help selectively and for important issues.
▷ Request job performance evaluations just to make sure you are meeting expectations.

The objective here is to stay on top of things at work and develop a support system that can be relied upon for years to come. The children will benefit because they have a father who is productive at work and has access to a variety of experienced parents who can help him make important decisions.

8. Informing Family and School

Informing the Family

Informing family members of the separation is like a double-edged sword. On the one hand, it can be a stressful experience because you are afraid of the reaction, yet on the other hand, you are finally able to tell someone and release this huge load from your shoulders. When I made the decision to separate, I knew it would come as a shock to my parents. I waited until all the legalities had been worked out before I told them. As I drove to my parent's house I remembered the special moments I had shared with my own father. My children deserved to have those memories as well. I made a point of setting aside an evening that would allow me to sit with them for a while and talk about it. This is too much of a change to announce over the phone. My parents were getting on in years and I thought it would be better if I could talk to them in person.

It is important to lay the ground rules for discussion of the separation. I asked my parents not to discuss the separation in the presence of my children. I knew that it would be quite possible that they could lay blame. I didn't want the children to hear their grandparents talking negatively about their mother.

As it turned out, my parents never did speak negatively about the children's mother. After the initial shock, they even had pleasant conversations with her, and she visited them on occasion. No negative remarks have ever been heard by the children that I'm aware of.

Very often family members will take sides in this type of situation. Family members who attempt to discredit one of the two parents are only raising the anxiety level of the children. Children of divorced parents definitely do not need to hear any of that. The last thing you need, no matter how angry you are, is for your children to have to choose which parent they love more. This can only bring about long-term emotional damage.

It is very important that the divorced father discourage remarks that may be upsetting to the children. It is important for the children to see their relatives on your side of the family, but if someone is badmouthing their mother, they will no longer want to visit that person. A divorced dad certainly doesn't want someone putting him down, so he should not be encouraging this in others. If tensions linger and there is a need for people to vent, create time with family when the children are not around. If you encourage disparaging remarks, chances are they will slip out when the children are around.

Informing the School

One of the first things a divorced father can do is inform their child's school about the separation. Asking them to keep a close eye on the children cannot hurt. At the same time, it is a good idea that they have the father's new phone number and address. This was one of the things that I neglected to do after I separated. Since I am a teacher, I was fortunate that many of the teachers as well as the principal of my children's school knew me. However, I should have made a more formal contact with the school myself.

Formal Contact

Making a formal contact with the school demonstrates that you care about how the children are feeling as well as how they are performing academically. Children who are depressed may withdraw or become more aggressive at school. One way to make this contact is to write a letter explaining the situation. I've known divorced fathers who have found these documents valuable when custody battles went to court. However, the communication should be rooted in a sincere desire to maintain contact with the school.

Another way to make contact is to go into the school and meet with the principal and the teachers. Make the point that you very much want to be kept informed of your child's progress. When I taught elementary school, I remember a divorced father who was very involved in his son's education. He consistently came to interviews and parent committee meetings. However, he did not have custody of his son. Eventually, he was able to gain custody of his child, and I believe that this was facilitated by his total involvement in the boy's schooling.

Stay Involved

Don't underestimate the power of being a part of your child's daily schedule. As much as possible, build your schedule around theirs. Slot them into your own busy schedule if you have to. They don't have to monopolize each day, but they need to feel that they are still of utmost importance to you. To do this try scheduling regular visits or phone calls to them.

I don't believe dragging custody battles out in court is productive for the children. However, a father has the right to equal time with his children. Divorced fathers should make a point of remaining an integral part of their children's lives. Our role is not limited to providing child support payments twice a month. I feel my children need me for so much more and I make a sincere attempt to meet these needs. Fathers who feel they do not have enough access to their own children must stay as involved as possible and fight for what is right if necessary.

9. Little Things that Can Mean a Lot

Telephone Directory

One of the most important items that I overlooked when I left the house was our personal telephone directory. It may seem like a small item, but it is a quick way to make contact with friends who may not know where to find you. Many of the friends had moved over the years, so I hadn't memorized their numbers. Many were in different cities as well.

In the early months following a separation, tensions can be quite high and calling for a telephone number could lead to more disagreement. As a result, I fell out of touch with people I had known for years. Fortunately, when I bumped into these people, they seemed genuinely happy to see me. Having a copy of the telephone directory will certainly help you keep in touch.

Friendships

Friendships can have a way of changing following a divorce. Most people don't choose sides, but there is usually someone who decides to make that choice. It is important to have friends around you during this tough time in your life. You will need to vent your frustrations at times and at other times you'll just need a good laugh. I hope I get to have fun with some of those friends I lost touch with as a result of the divorce. However, I will have to take the initiative.

The unfortunate part about my error in judgment was that in the early months following the divorce, my children never saw me interacting with these friends. They sometimes asked how come I did not speak to certain people anymore. I remember answering that I was not happy that those friends were not there for me when I needed help. I'm not sure that was a very good answer, but it was an honest answer about how I felt. I believe that it was important for them to hear me express my feelings. They seemed to accept the answer and didn't push the point too much. Ideally, maintaining friendships provides continuity both for you and the children. It is just another connection to their former life that is probably comforting to them. Fortunately, I did have some good friends around me, and I eventually did reach out and called an old friend who has been very good to me.

Change of Address

Something I did manage to do quickly was provide the post office with a change of address. All my mail could be rerouted to my new place. If you have to pick up your mail, then you will have to go to your former wife's house every day. That may not be something you want to do. You need to establish a new mailing address and you need to make a break from daily visits.

If you have left the home, you really have given up the right to be showing up there on a daily basis. At a certain point, this could be considered harassment, or maybe your wife will misinterpret this as an invitation to reconcile. Your former wife has a right to move on with her life as well.

She may not appreciate her former husband showing up all the time.

Scheduled Visits

Your children will also get confused about what is going on if you are showing up at their mother's house constantly. It won't be long before they're saying, "Maybe Mom and Dad are getting back together!" Make the parameters of your visits very clear so there is no confusion in their minds about what is going on between you and their mother.

Documents

When you leave it is important to take with you personal financial records including outstanding credit–card bills. These are all records that you will eventually have to share with lawyers or courts. You don't want to have to go back to the house for them after you have left, particularly if the situation is tense. You will need to get permission from your former wife to do that once you have left.

Assume that the locks will be changed, and you won't be permitted access any longer. Think carefully about your personal files and take what you need.

Copies of any insurance policies or deeds for property are also important. You will also need your birth certificate and passport if you have one. Sometimes these items can be overlooked when emotions are running high. I was happy to have copies of bills and bank statements with me, if only so I could inform companies of my new address.

Cut Credit Cards

Credit card confusion can get nasty if you have not worked

this out with your former wife. Credit cards are usually in one name, but often two people use them. Make sure you distribute debt and get separate cards prior to the separation. The separation agreement should stipulate that you are individually responsible for any debt either of you accrued on the cards. You do not want to be stuck with a credit card that both of you used that has a huge outstanding balance in your name.

Utility Companies

In addition to making sure that the credit card situation is straightened out, it is also important to notify local utility companies that you have moved. You don't want to be paying for utilities in two places at the same time. Make sure that your separation agreement specifies when all these changes take place or arrange a mutually acceptable date with your former wife for the switchover.

This is one of the reasons why it is always better to have a legal separation. Everything is laid out in black and white so that there are no misunderstandings. Make the phone calls yourself so that you know your name is deleted at the old address and added to the new one.

Family Memories

On a more personal note, one item that I had kept since the children were little was a portfolio of many of the things that they had done over the years, such as pieces of art and kindergarten reports. I had put them away in folders in a filing cabinet. Unfortunately, with the anxiety of the separation and leaving the house, I overlooked those folders and left them there. However, I'm sure the children will find them some day and be happily surprised.

It is important to bring photographs of the children with you. It provides a connection for you and the children with a life that they will always remember. It is important that you reflect on that life in a positive light, so that they see that it was a special time for you as well. Unfortunately, I left a number of photographs of the children at their mother's house. At this particular time, I am probably able to get copies of these photographs because the relationship with my former wife is good.

My children have fond memories of our family together when they were younger. When she was in grade ten, my daughter gave me a poem about one of those memories.

The Robin Hood Tree

The Robin Hood Tree
Was what we all used to call it
The fort of safety, where we all enjoyed sanctuary
From the Sheriff of Nottingham
My neighbors would arrive every morning
To play Robin Hood
Prepared with our toy bows and arrows
We'd scatter to the golf course
Hide in our citadel and
Prepare for the attack...
Suddenly our newly fortified fathers came out of the
Woods
Advancing for the strike

And capture my army of friends!
In days gone by
Life's biggest concern was
Who'd win the next battle
Yet I still return to the Robin Hood Tree
For the lure of protection

We make a point of reminiscing about vacations, special events, and other occasions from years gone by. Pictures can be a fun way to reflect on the happy times from the past. It is probably time for me to request some of those pictures from their younger days.

Since we're talking about pictures, do your children walk into your house and see pictures of themselves? By placing pictures up around your apartment, you are giving your children a reminder of how important they are to you each time they come over to your place. Your children will notice everything that you do. To make the transition easier, I also put a picture of their mother in their bedroom. Years later, the picture still sits in my daughter's room.

Videotapes
Today many people vidcotape their children during special events or at certain stages in their lives. Their mother and I made a number of these videos when the children were younger. I haven't seen these in years. If you know that such videos exist then it would be wise to get copies made. Kids love looking at old videos of themselves when they were little. My children bring them over occasionally, but I should get copies for myself.

Rewriting Your Will

One of the things that I decided to do immediately following the divorce was to write a new will. My assets were not that great, but I was still sensitive to the fact that the children would have to be looked after financially should something happen to me. I visited a lawyer, re-wrote my will based on my new circumstances, and made my sister and brother-in-law executors.

10. Dealing with Rumors and Opinions

Often, third parties that know nothing about the circumstances surrounding the separation decide to add their two cents' worth. Everyone seems to love a soap opera, and when you are going through something like this, you are living it. If, through the children or another party, you hear that negative things are being said about you by someone in your former wife's family, it is important that you address this with her. You cannot demand that people not have an opinion on the separation. As the children's father, however, it is quite reasonable that you request that nothing negative be said about you in front of the children. Sometimes, simply sending a signal that you know what is being said is enough to stop the misinformation.

You Couldn't Do Anything Right Anyway
Sometimes the distress that follows a separation only serves as fuel for embers that have been waiting to burn more brightly. In other words, you couldn't do anything right in this particular person's eyes anyway, and now there is a real excuse to put you down. A good tactic would be to sit the children down and explain the situation to them in language they can understand. Does the person making the remarks have another reason why he/she wants to try and hurt you?

The children may not be able to understand why the person is upset with you. Since you won't know everything that has been said, make sure you remind the children that you love them more than anything. Another good point to discuss with them is that some people react very differently when they are hurt. A person who is saying negative things about a father may really be saying that they are disappointed the marriage did not work.

Your Reaction Counts

Threats and obscenities on a father's part can only create further turmoil within the family in general and the children specifically. Your children are going to hear things elsewhere and comment. It is important not to have a knee-jerk reaction to information that is shared with you through the children. Show them that you can listen and be thoughtful. Remember, they will probably make the comment specifically to see your reaction.

I know that I was hurt by comments that I heard second-hand. After years of marriage this is a natural feeling. However, as a father I want to be considered a good role model for my children. A failed marriage does not mean I have failed as a father. As divorced fathers we must continue to manifestly practice our parenting skills to retain our natural right as fathers.

Hopefully, after many years our children will be able to look back and appreciate the effort that their father made to give them a healthier and happier life.

When dealing with rumors remember these points:

▷People who perpetrate falsehoods or negative comments are usually unhappy themselves.

▷Don't let the children see you react in anger if they share something with you.

▷ Sometimes a kind word about the person who made the remark will diffuse the whole situation. (For example, "I like Auntie Maude. It's too bad she doesn't understand.")

▷Remain consistent and sincere and comments will decrease.

▷ As time passes the "soap opera" you have been living will be of less interest to people.

▷ Your children will remember the quality of the interactions with their parents—both of them— above everything else.

11. Creating a Home

Where to Begin?

During the two-week period at my sister and brother-in-law's home, other topics of discussion began to creep into the conversation. For instance, I found out that they both had an interest in toll painting, antiques, and stained glass. They were hobbies that both enjoyed very much, and I began to take an interest and learn more about each. I had more time on my hands, so I began to read a little about these various hobbies of theirs. I thought that maybe this was a way to begin decorating my apartment. However, I knew there was no way that I could afford to hire a decorator and buy all kinds of antiques.

The best way to avoid putting oneself into serious debt following a separation is to think before you leap. My sister suggested that garage sales would be a great place to consider buying things. I had absolutely nothing, so I couldn't help but to agree that it just might work. There was no way that I wanted to get into the buy now/pay later trap. I knew that I would not have any more money later. However, considering carefully how to proceed with the apartment was one of the best decisions I ever made.

Release the Tension

Another of the great benefits of staying at my sister's house was that each night after dinner we would take the time to go on long walks. Considering the ordeal that I had just been through, I found this a most relaxing experience. Going on these walks seemed to recharge my batteries. The fresh air and the discussions about trivial things were invigorating. I could feel the tension leaving my body as my mind cleared itself of thoughts of divorce.

Increasingly, I found myself thinking of my apartment. Up until this time I hadn't really dealt with the reality of being alone. I began to realize that I did not even own a fork. I didn't have a plan to determine how I was going to bring all this together. However, it was going to be important that the place would be a comfortable home for the three of us and I was determined to put my imprint on it.

Make Priorities

Since I had just left a household full of beautiful furnishings, I was determined not to settle for just anything that came along. I wanted to put some thought into the process of furnishing the apartment. I made the decision to take as much time as I needed rather than buy anything that appeared to be a good price. Of course every individual has to determine when and what they need for themselves. I knew that I would have more time on my hands, and I'm the type of person that likes to keep busy. Keeping focused on this would occupy my time. Any type of constructive activity that is designed to help rebuild your life and get your mind off the stressful separation process can be extremely therapeutic.

The walks with my sister and brother-in-law each evening made it perfectly clear to me that it was time to start rebuilding. They were helping me think about what to do next. For the first time in a long time I was getting excited about something and it felt good. Whether I succeeded or failed would rest squarely on my own shoulders. There would be no one else to blame but myself if things went wrong.

Keep the Children in Mind

The decisions I would make would always have the children in mind. A divorced father has a responsibility to his children first. He does not have the freedom to look after his own needs all the time. During this rebuilding process, I tried to keep the children's needs as a priority at all times.

Take Inventory

When furnishing an apartment or home it is obviously important to take inventory of what you own. I was determined to get by as frugally as I could in the beginning. In other words, don't spend money on items that you don't need immediately. The expenses following a separation can be unbelievable, so it is wise to avoid items that are not absolutely necessary. In time, one can accumulate things, but it is absolutely foolhardy to put yourself in extreme debt needlessly.

Recycle

I got an old dresser that was being thrown out in the garbage. I decided that I could use it for the children's room if I could fix it up. I did not have anything for my own bedroom except the comforter. I did get an old table that the kids used to color on in our basement. I decided I could use that for a short while as a kitchen table. I ended up using it for five-and-a-half years. I owned absolutely nothing that could be used in the bathroom and the kitchen. For the living room, I had a sofa, a lamp, and a picture. So there was plenty to be worried about.

Prioritize

Beds were an immediate concern, and one has to be quite careful about buying second–hand beds. I was not prepared to do that, but a close friend did have a twin bed that she gave me. Unfortunately, I had to buy a bed for myself as well as another twin bed for my daughter. However, the upside was that I would have the beds for years to come. Actually, once I had beds for all of us, I felt great. Mind you, we had nothing that would keep us warm, but at that point it seemed like a big accomplishment for me. I was quite proud of myself but yet quickly realized that I had barely even begun.

Health and Safety Items

If you are a father living alone and have children of different ages, then you would be wise to stock up on products for the cleanliness, health and safety of the children. For instance, if the children come over and accidentally cut themselves, do you have bandages in the apartment? This is something I thought of before I got the apartment. On my initial "stock-up" visit to the pharmacy I picked up some extra toothbrushes for the kids as well as other items. Your children need to be reassured that you still care.

This is a very simple way of expressing that you are still thinking of them even when you are not with them. Think of your place as their home as well. By having items that are theirs that stay in the apartment, they eventually begin to think of it as their home too.

You can anticipate their needs as the children get older. For instance, will you need more shampoo or soap when the children are there? If you have teenage daughters, is there a supply of tampons in their room? Is the apartment welcoming and clean when they arrive at your place? A little foresight on your part will reap rewards over time. Be patient and don't try to buy their affection. It will be the little things that you do that bring them closer to you emotionally.

Home Entertainment

It soon occurred to me that I had no "entertainment system" at all. I had left everything in their mother's home. Now, I happen to watch very little television, but I knew the children would need one. Our stereo was where I spent most of my time at home, and that was now gone. Second–hand bargains can be ideal for these types of items. Fortunately, I have a friend who has an audio/video store. Through him, I was able to get some equipment that had either been demos or traded–in at the store. These were all bought at a very reasonable price and are still working after six years. Later, I found similar equipment at garage sales that I would have bought but I didn't need.

Home entertainment is an important area because these are items that the children will probably use. The problem is that it is easy to get mesmerized by all the fancy equipment available and end up going into debt quickly. Make yourself a budget before you go into a store in order to avoid spending too much money.

Children's Room

Fortunately, my mother had some old sheets she wasn't using that I could use for the twin beds. A visit to Costco nailed down pillows, comforters, and blinds for their rooms. All this only cost me about $100.00. A friend gave me an old trunk that I used in the children's room for their toys. The old dresser I had was of high quality, so my sister repainted it for me. We used the colors in the comforters and the blinds. For the first time in my life, I was learning what decorating was all about and I was actually enjoying it. The children's room was the priority and it was beginning to take shape.

Using Available Time Wisely

Since I had access to a large garage at my sister's house, I was able to work on pieces of furniture there. I stripped down the top of the old table and put a finish on it that could withstand everyday use. I bought some wooden chairs at Wal-Mart that I put together myself. I purposely paid very little for these as I thought I would eventually replace them. However, they are still in use today. If I had more time, I would have bought chairs at a garage sale. I did not have that luxury. Garage sale bargains usually come unexpectedly, but there were no chairs available at the time. We needed something to sit around the table for dinner and I was determined that we would do that each night the children were over.

Apartment Problems

The day finally came when I got the key and went by myself to visit the apartment. This was something I was told not to do by the counselor. He had stated that it was probably a good idea to visit the apartment with friends for the first time. I figured I could handle it, so I decided to go anyway. My excitement was soon turned to devastation when I saw the state of the place. It was filthy. The tenant had hidden the dirt well behind the furniture. Everything would need to be painted. And I had asked for the floor to be refinished, and they hadn't touched it.

This was a shock for me and it was the first time I really wondered what I had done with my life. I had never lived in an apartment so I wasn't prepared for the landlord/tenant relationship. I just believed that if you say you're going to do something you do it. If you're going to move into a rental apartment, get things put in writing. I was quite discouraged and the reality of the situation I had put myself in was painfully obvious. The place I was going to live in was a mess. I felt very much alone.

The next day they were painting in the apartment, but the floors were not started. I asked if they were painting the kitchen cupboards, and they said yes. So I was frustrated that the floors weren't done, but relieved that the dirty cupboards were going to be painted. Things were looking up!

About six days after my lease had started the floors

were done. I could begin moving things into the place. This too was a mistake because they were still patching up something on my kitchen ceiling. Months later I eventually noticed that some sports memorabilia that I had collected was missing. That was the only time it could have been taken.

Finally, I went to ask the landlord when the cupboards were going to be painted. (It was his son who said they were to be done.) He looked at me as if I was crazy. He commented that he had no intention of painting the cupboards and could not care less that it was six days after the lease took effect and I had still not been able to move in. Although angry, I realized quickly that I couldn't trust these people or rely on them at all. From then on, I would take care of things on my own in the apartment.

In the meantime the kids needed to know I was still around. I made a point of calling them regularly and bringing them over to my sister's house. The connection to my family was a good thing for them. It took their minds off the situation. At this point they believed I didn't call enough. I got the feeling that I couldn't help but be portrayed as the "bad guy" because I had left the home. So there were pros and cons to the decision to have them stay in the house.

However, they got to stay with friends and in the home they grew up in. But on the other hand, I was the one who left, and I was not sure they would ever get over that. It is important to consider whether to have the kids stay in the home with their mother or sell the house and move elsewhere. Ideally, strictly from a father's point of view, it would be great if they were able to stay in the home with their father, but I believe that seldom happens. They will definitely be more comfortable in the surroundings they grew up in. Remember, they have their stuff there and the memories of a family that has separated but they may still wish that their parents were back together.

This issue of whether the children will stay in their own home or relocate is a delicate one. As a father, if we leave the home, I believe we are perceived as abandoning the family. It is an impression held by society, which is reinforced by government agencies such as schools and upheld in divorce courts all over. The father is usually asked to pay and that is very often considered enough. The welfare of the child and the relationship with the father is ignored. This is one instance where it is believed that money can buy happiness. There is little concern for the fact that a child may be kept from his/her father. It is extremely important that no matter what financial settlement you eventually agree upon, you have unlimited access to your children.

12. Look after Yourself

Keeping a Diary

It may be important to keep a diary or journal, particularly during the early months following the separation. I was nervous and unsure how things would work out with the children. It would be helpful to have this record if you anticipate a visit to court. You certainly want to avoid court if at all possible. However, situations can change quickly and you should be as prepared as possible. The problem is there are so many things that you are trying to remember at this time that it is impossible to recall all the incidents that come up concerning the children.

Some of the things you may wish to record in the diary could be the dates you have the children. Another might be parental agreements with their mother regarding custody and other settlements. You might want to record activities you did with the kids. Disagreements over particular issues with your former wife could be recorded in the journal.

As the children grow up, they may want to spend more time with you or their mother. How will you work this out? If their mother or you have a live–in boyfriend or girlfriend, the children may want out. If you are truly interested in doing the right thing for your children, the journal will reflect those thoughts. As future situations arise, a detailed journal can be very helpful in clarifying what has gone on in the past.

Doctor's Checkup

Another good thing to do in the early months following the separation is to see a doctor. You've been under a lot of stress, so it is a good time to have a complete physical. Unfortunately, a few months following the separation I got physically sick from a parasite in my intestinal system. Over a one-month period I lost about twenty pounds. This is a good time to know your body. I saw a few doctors; each one prescribed sleeping pills or anti-depressants. Although I was nervous during the lead-up and the separation, by the time I got the apartment running to my satisfaction, I was much better emotionally after the separation than before, so it didn't make any sense to me. I decided to not take the pills.

Finally, I saw a doctor who right away asked whether I had been under any emotional stress lately. I explained the situation to her and then requested that some lab tests be done to determine the problem. A friend of mine was a nurse working at the clinic. She alerted me when the lab results were in and had the doctor on the line with a prescription ready. I started to feel better within days.

Regular Checkups

You want to be around as long as you can for your children, so a regular doctor's check–up is a good idea. Actually you may even want to tell your children that you had a check–up and the doctor said you were in great shape. This can only make them feel more secure about the fact that you will be a part of their lives for a long time. Besides, if you are relatively healthy you can do more activities with your children. And the younger they are, the more they want you to do things with them.

My family doctor sat me down after my physical. I had told him about the separation. He explained the need to take precautions in sexual relations and obviously recommended condoms. He made a point of saying that blood tests were easy to do if a partner came along who I was serious about.

Your doctor is a great resource at this time in your life. Protect yourself as much as possible and know your own body. Remember, you will probably be living alone for a while. You don't need to react to every ache and pain, but you don't want anything to linger for too long either. A lot of people feel they can deal with everything. However, there are times you will need medical help. You don't want bronchitis to turn into pneumonia if you can avoid it. Respect your body and take care of it. Remember, time is money and if you can't spend time at work, you're going to be short of money.

13. Financial Issues

Your financial situation will not be what it was no matter what tax bracket you are in. However, the average divorced father has some serious problems to contend with at this time. Chances are, your income has stayed the same yet your expenses have dramatically increased. You now have child support payments to contend with on top of everything else.

Think Ahead

It may be difficult when you are emotionally distraught, but now is a good time to get a clear picture of your new financial quandary. You may want to meet with a financial planner if your finances are more complicated. Otherwise, take a good look at monthly income and expenses. You will probably have to work extra hard at keeping yourself in a "financial comfort zone".

Chance for Advancement

Obviously, assessing your job situation is an excellent way to assess potential improvements to your income. Are you in a "dead-end job"? In other words, you are not able to climb any higher in the company that you are presently employed. However, be careful of too much change in the early years following a divorce. Friends at work who are supportive to your emotional needs may be worth much more than a small increase in pay.

Financial Stress

Immediately following the separation, you will probably be under a fair amount of financial stress. This is a good time to reflect on your financial stability. This, of course, may raise your anxiety or reduce it depending on what you conclude. If your anxiety is raised, you will have to develop a plan of action that will help alleviate it.

If there is a consistent amount of money coming in each month then only so much can go out. To think any differently can only lead to bankruptcy.

Particularly following a separation, the average dad will be extremely strapped for cash. You must be very patient and think clearly when making even the smallest financial decisions. The reason for this is that financial stress will seriously affect your relationship with your children. This is a time for adjustment and you will be better off restricting your lifestyle so it better reflects your financial restraints.

Your children may also have to be made aware that things will be different. They should not be made to feel guilty and you certainly don't want to make them fearful of not having enough money for basic things such as food or clothing. This is a delicate topic, but it is crucial to long-term financial stability.

Insurance Plans

Another thing that may indirectly help you and your children is a re-evaluation of your insurance plans if you have any. You may be paying too much for very little coverage. You don't want to eliminate your insurance coverage. As a matter of fact, you want to make sure your children will be taken care of should something happen to you. However, the biggest hurdle you have in the short term is to free up cash for everyday living. How high are the premiums that you are presently paying? Any amount you can save, through comparison shopping, will help you deal with expenses.

For instance, maybe you are paying for an expensive whole–life insurance plan when you can get the same coverage in a far cheaper term insurance plan. Ask friends or a financial advisor. It doesn't cost anything to ask. An insurance broker will hunt down the most inexpensive plan for free.

Transportation

One of the things you want to resist doing is going out and buying a fancy sports car or something similar. The idea here is to try and decrease expenses, not increase debt. I know a divorced dad who did just that after his divorce when his house was sold. It is now ten years later and he still drives the car, but he'll never be able to buy his own home again. In the meantime, he had to rent a one-bedroom apartment that made it difficult when his son came over. His car expenses prevented him from taking advantage of sagging home prices in our area over a five-year period. His decision to purchase the car shaped his future as a divorced dad. There was little money left to spend on his son, to go on vacation, or to buy clothes for himself. He could have improved his financial future by investing the proceeds from his home wisely. He might even be driving a new sports car today if he had used discipline ten years ago.

At the time of my separation, I had an eight-year old BMW. I kept driving it for two more years. At that time, I had to consider safety for my children when transporting them around in a ten-year old car. In addition, I had to consider the expense of maintaining and repairing the car. I opted to sell it, despite my fondness for it, and ended up leasing a Toyota Corolla. The monthly payments were reasonable and the car provided a safe and dependable automobile for the children and me for the next four years.

It also gave me a clear picture of what my car expenses would be for the next four years. It was important to choose a car that would accommodate two growing teenagers, their friends, and me. This is a good, simple way to remind the children that there is always room for them in your life. If you have more than one child, a two-seater sports car sends a clear and disturbing message to them.

When purchasing a car, remember to check with the insurance company to see which model is actually cheaper to insure. There can be a huge difference. With the price of gasoline today, you want to consider a vehicle that is going to be quite economical. Remember, as the children get older they become more mobile. It is important to know where they are and whom they are with at any given time. Your car is going to allow you to do that.

If you live in an area where public transportation is readily available, then transportation may not be a problem.

In that case, you may be able to avoid buying a vehicle altogether. However, if you are like most of us, you will need something to get around.

You can't underestimate how important your car will be to you and the children. You will have to be able to drive to their mother's home if you are going to have any hope of seeing the kids on a regular basis. You will have to be able to get to their school and other activities that they are involved in. You cannot do that if your car is constantly breaking down or you cannot afford to buy gasoline. With divorce, your disposable income has been depleted and gasoline prices are on the rise, so by thinking economically you will be giving yourself the opportunity to spend more time with your children.

Since you will be living outside the home where your children spend most of their time, the car becomes much more important to all of you. If you like to camp, consider the type of vehicle you will need so you can spend valuable vacation time with the children. I coached my son's baseball team, so I had to have a trunk big enough to hold all the gear. The purchase of the right car requires considerable thought for a whole variety of reasons.

Purchasing a Home?
If you do sell a property and have some money from the sale, it can be very tempting to buy another property. However, it is important to get grounded emotionally and financially before taking on the extra burden of home ownership. Owning and maintaining a home requires time and money and although initially appealing, it may actually prove

burdensome to you after awhile. Your children will need your attention and that will be a difficult thing to give them if you are spending all your time and money looking after a house. After my separation, I was quite happy not to have to worry about shoveling snow or cutting lawns for a little while. I could concentrate on the children and plan a path for the future without getting bogged down in home repairs. We would eventually get to that house, but I had to rebuild my life in incremental steps in order to get there.

I know of a dad who bought a house immediately following the separation. The difficulty with that was that he was still grieving the failure of his marriage. Unfortunately, he did not have the motivation, the heart, or the finances required in order to maintain the house. He bought it with good intentions. He wanted a home for his two children. However, it ended up being just one more thing that was bringing him down. He was feeling emotionally drained and he hadn't calculated his decreased income because of child–support payments. He had not been thinking clearly enough and ended up barely getting by both financially and emotionally.

My suggestion is to do very little for a while in terms of purchasing a home. Look at your first place as temporary until you are able to get your bearings. You don't know how long it will take to get yourself back on your feet again. I spent the first few years making sure my kids and I were okay emotionally. The divorce had left scars, but they were healing and quality time together was helping.

Constant worries about house problems and financial difficulties can prevent you from healing emotionally.

Being patient and thinking things through allowed me to feel better with time. That does not mean that I didn't get frustrated occasionally. There were many emotional valleys along the way but the valleys eventually become less frequent. I know I am a stronger and more confident person than I was six years ago.

As a father, I just want my kids to do the best that they can in life and to be happy. Having parents who are divorced does not have to prevent those two things from happening. However, if these goals are ever to be achieved, a dad must be involved and committed to his children. Child–support payments are no substitute for active involvement. You owe it to your children to be the best father possible. They will only be children once and this is your opportunity to be there with them. No one has a magic formula or can guarantee perfection—you only have your knowledge and intuition as a parent to guide you. Parenting is a lot easier if you are able to place yourself on solid ground both emotionally and financially. Getting yourself back on that solid ground should be a priority following a divorce.

14. Dealing with Your Expenses

There is always the temptation to go out and spend money once you have separated. You probably left a lot in the house and took very little with you. However, the best thing you can do for yourself is to limit expenses during this period.

Plan your purchases carefully. Here are some guidelines you can follow that will help:

▷ Do not try and get everything at once.

▷ Avoid using credit cards because they can accumulate debt just as fast as it takes you to take one out of your wallet.

▷ Look for sales on practical house items like towels, sheets, and utensils.

▷ Stay clear of "buy now, pay later" schemes. What makes you think you are going to have more money later?

▷ Be aware of the interest you pay on credit cards and loans.

▷ Try to come up with a plan for decorating your new place. This allows you to be selective and avoid impulse buying. As well, it can keep you busy in a healthy and constructive way following the separation.

Rely on friends to give you advice concerning items you may have never considered before. I had never thought twice about what two hundred-thread-count on sheets meant until I asked my sister. Now, when I look for sheets on sale I check to make sure the thread count is two hundred or more if I want quality. Friends were able to steer me to both boutiques and dollar stores where value could be found. However, whenever I shopped at expensive shops, I always looked for "seconds" or excellent sales. It is important to avoid paying full price if at all possible.

Debt

One of the major obstacles you are going to have to face prior to getting your life back on track is your debt load. Debt can multiply quickly particularly following a divorce. You may be carrying debt that goes back years into your marriage. I know I had one loan of $8000 that I had to pay off. That was in addition to credit–card debt.

The debt load can increase dramatically if legal fees are heaped on top of them. Purchases for your new place can quickly bury you. The first step in helping yourself is to recognize that your debt load may be too heavy. Begin to think of ways to ease the burden. Consolidation of loans comes to mind. This should lower your monthly payments. Sometimes relatives may be in a position to help you out.

Debt has to be reassessed regularly. I was continuously exploring all my options. You may be in a position to sell something of value that will help you out. Bankruptcy should be avoided at all costs as it affects your ability to obtain funds for other things later on. Your credit rating is destroyed and many future doors are closed for you. Ideally, you want to be financially creative with your limited funds so that you are actually improving your credit rating. In the end, however, the only way to improve the rating is simple: meet payment deadlines.

Bartering

One way that you can help your financial situation is to try bartering services with other people. For instance, if your children need tutoring and you can't afford it then maybe you can offer a service in exchange for the tutoring. As an example, if you are a painter, there may be a teacher who is willing to tutor your children in exchange for some painting. An accountant could offer that service in exchange for dental work. Many professionals might be happy to offer their services to someone who would do their gardening. You are not restricted because of your profession. Actually, the more creative you are, the more successful you will become at bartering. You will definitely have to put more time and effort into tapping into some of these resources. You can't depend on opportunities to just fall into your lap. You'll have to create some opportunities for yourself and you may have to be aggressive.

Reputation

Your reputation as a skilled and dependable person will help or hinder you when attempting to tap into bartering relationships. Whether you are a professional golfer or a maintenance worker, you are constantly leaving impressions with people. If you have made a good impression, chances are that your skills may be of use to them. Therefore, the combination of your reputation and your skill level may place you in a position to generate income. Reputations are developed over years and are based on the perceptions of family, friends, and colleagues. You must continue to nurture a positive perception by others if you want to make life better for you and your children.

Increasing Revenue

Revenue from your present job is a known entity. It is the potential of the unknown that I am talking about. Here is an example. A friend of mine started going to garage sales every Saturday morning. He noticed that whenever he went to a sale, sports items were always selling cheap compared to store prices. He bought his son and daughter skates and bikes. He eventually found out that a second hand sports store would pay him for equipment that he found. He quickly used his sales skills to find out what the store needed and proceeded to hunt at garage sales. Within no time he was making up to $300 or $400 on a Saturday morning.

Part time employment

Another way to get extra money is to get a part–time job. Be careful though—you want it to accommodate the kids' schedule, so you can spend more time with them. Make it clear to your employer that you are unavailable when you have your kids. Your time with them is the most valuable investment you can make, so you don't want to jeopardize that. The job doesn't have to be sophisticated. In fact it may be mindless but give you something to do. You do not want to be working so hard that you are too tired to spend quality time with the children. If you find that happening then you are defeating the purpose and your life will become more chaotic as the children begin to rebel.

Use Your Home!

Working out of your own home may be another option you want to explore. It might let you declare certain expenses in the house as income tax deductions. The Internet has provided many people with job opportunities right out of their own homes. If you have skills in this area then it is probably worth exploring. It also allows for flexibility in your schedule so that you adjust your time on the computer around the children's schedule.

Garage Sales

I've explored many of the varied ways to increasing income that I have described. The one that I enjoyed the most was the garage sale route. Each time I purchased an item at far less than its retail value, I considered it an increase to my income. A dollar saved at a garage sale would, in effect, be increasing my income. In other words, there would be more money left for other priorities such as the children and savings.

I no longer owned any tools, so I made a point of collecting them at fifty cents to a dollar. I spent thirty to forty dollars for about $400 worth of tools. Kitchen utensils were readily available as well. Some furniture and other household items were picked up over time. We often believe that "new" is the only way to go. However, when you stop and think about it, a ten-year old pair of pliers can work just as well as a new pair.

As I sit here in my dining room, I see many items that were purchased at garage sales. There is an old scale that sits on the windowsill for decoration that was purchased for a few dollars. Beside the scale is a wrought–iron candleholder that was found for one dollar. Behind me is a stained–glass lamp that needed some work, but only cost two dollars. My sister repaired it, and I've been told it is worth about $150.

It is not always easy to find the things you want at a garage sale. Things like curtains may not match what you need, so you may have to look elsewhere. I used to bring my kids with me to the garage sales and we would make an adventure out of it. Often, they would find a small toy or book that they wanted and it would only cost twenty-five cents. I found a bicycle for me for twenty-five dollars that I later found out had sold new for $500.

Furnishing the New Place

Most of the furniture that I ended up buying for my apartment was either second–hand or antique. "Old" was the theme, and I decided not to settle for anything I didn't like. I was prepared to be patient rather than rush out and get something just for the sake of filling up the apartment. I am still using the table that I finished in my sister's garage. I have a bookcase that had been painted orange and a friend was going to throw out. I stripped it down, refinished it, and had glass cut to fit the doors. That was a freebee and most people comment on it as soon as they come into the place.

Another beautiful piece is a buffet that sits in the dining room. It was in a friend's basement filled with board games. My friend gave it to me and all I had to do with it was put oil on it to restore its original luster. Another friend sold me two chairs she had for forty dollars. One was a 1920s wingback chair that I reupholstered. That was an expensive thing to do, but you just can't find furniture of that quality anymore, so I thought it was a good investment.

15. Find out What You Need to Help You Heal

Refinishing Furniture (Therapy for the Mind and Soul)
The whole process of finding and then refinishing furniture became a form of therapy for me. Obviously, I had more time to myself following the separation. I wanted to use this time in a positive way. It could be easy to spend free time grieving and accomplishing very little. However, that will not benefit you or your children.

This is an important time to reflect but also to move on and begin a new life for you and your children in a productive way. Your mind can play tricks on you if it is idle for too long. One divorced father that I know had finally settled all the details of the divorce with his former wife, but he couldn't let the disagreements end. He didn't have something to take up his time other than the preoccupation with the animosity between him and his former wife. He began sending her inappropriate messages either through chat rooms on the Internet or e-mail. He was aware that he was doing something wrong, but he couldn't stop himself. Well, to make a long story short, the police eventually showed up at his door and he was charged with harassment.

Hurt, anger and frustration are normal during this period. It is how you control those emotions that will make the difference between the possibility of having an ongoing positive relationship with your children or not. You will lose any opportunity to have a stable and productive relationship with your children if you are unable to control your own actions. If these strong emotions are directing your actions inappropriately then seek out some professional assistance before the damage done is too great.

It is important to find something else to occupy both your time and your thoughts. Repairing pieces of furniture that I found for the apartment helped me do that. The impending separation had been on my mind for so long, it was difficult to shift my focus in another direction. This concrete exercise provided a distraction from the grieving process I had been going through for a couple of years. The physical exertion involved in that type of activity was also a great way to release energy. I have heard it said that if one keeps physically active then the chances of being depressed are diminished.

Tangible Reward

My preoccupation with refinishing furniture also gave me a form of instant gratification. The reward for my effort was quite tangible, and I suggest choosing something that will give you some short-term reward as well. Be careful about choosing something that is never-ending. When I completed a project, I had something new to add to the apartment. My sister and my brother-in-law offered suggestions while I was working in their garage. It is much better to have people around you for support. When I brought the piece of furniture home, the children were usually excited about it too!

Involve the Children

Eventually, my son and daughter began to offer their own opinions on what was still needed in the apartment. We were going to garage sales together to find things. I believe they could see that this apartment we had was evolving into a home. But more importantly, they saw that their father was going to be okay. Even though their life following the divorce was going to be different, they realized that Dad was still going to be there for them.

Decorating

I never would have believed that I would ever be interested in Martha Stewart decorating tips. I had never paid any attention to this prior to the divorce. Decorating may not be something you are interested in, but it was another way for me to get my son and daughter involved and feel more at home in their new surroundings. Remember, the children will not be as comfortable in a new place initially. This can be frustrating for you.

At the time of the separation my son was turning eight and my daughter eleven, yet they were very keen to choose the colors for their bedroom. They even wanted to try some of the painting. They were quite happy with the finished product. They picked out some blinds for their room that matched the comforters on their beds. Incidentally, window coverings can add up very quickly, so keep it simple and as cheap as possible.

Within a year of getting the apartment, my daughter could see that we had an antique theme happening. She suggested we do a stenciling around the ceiling throughout the living room area. I had no idea what stenciling was, so I consulted with my sister and a friend of mine who is a part–time decorator.

Once I had the information I needed, my daughter and I drove to a major hardware chain that carried stencil products. My daughter chose the colors to match the curtains and the furniture in the room. This helped tremendously since I am partially color-blind.

The great thing about this project was that it was my daughter's idea. She felt comfortable providing input into what she felt was needed in the apartment. She was very impressed with the finished product and it was there for us to enjoy every day.

Don't Ignore Emotional Needs

This preoccupation with concrete items and tasks cannot be allowed to deflect your attention from the emotional needs that your children may have at this time. You still have to be there for them as a father and provide emotional support as needed.

Most of the time I spent refinishing furniture occurred when the children were not with me. You will have your children for a limited amount of time. You don't want to be working every time they come over. If that happens, they won't want to come over anymore. It is different, of course, if you are doing the activity together, and they are keen to be a part of it. The key is to continue to be a dad and to enjoy your children when you have them. After all, they'll only be this age once. Why miss it?

The Roller Coaster Ride

Once you are in that new place and you have accumulated some basics, you can begin the process of rebuilding your life. The emotional roller coaster ride that you have been on is probably still underway. When I first moved into the apartment, I was so uptight that I used to jump each time the telephone rang. The emotional valleys that will haunt you can take a while to diminish in frequency. Things will get better over time if you do not let guilt control your feelings. You can't be running over to your children's home each time the phone rings. You have to live a more independent life when your children are not with you.

You will never be able to fully ignore what is going on in your former wife's home. However, you can't try to manage what is going on in the two homes. You have to move on and manage your own home just as their mother has to manage hers. A divorced father needs time to heal emotionally as well. Maybe we forget that at times because we are so used to masking our feelings.

Accept the Change

In time, everyone in the family will have to adjust to the new situation. There is no use trying to pretend that things haven't changed. I realized early on that if I tried to take care of things happening in both homes, I would be emotionally drained. My children had two competent parents who were perfectly capable of sharing the burden of the variety of situations that arose. The children still needed a strong parent in each home. I believed that we would both have to feel good about our decision to be the best possible parents for our children.

Dealing with the "Guilt" Factor

You will have to deal with the guilt that often accompanies a family break-up. Some fathers and mothers spoil their children in an attempt to compensate. Others frequently take the children to restaurants to make visits more palatable. Many let discipline slide because they want the time spent with their children to be positive. In fact, each of these situations is artificially created because of guilt over the divorce.

A child doesn't need everything, doesn't want to go out for dinner each day, and definitely needs to be disciplined. They need their father. That means that their dad is going to have to say "no" once in a while just like before. They are in a new situation so it is very important to make the parameters clear.

The Guilt Test

I remember distinctly when my daughter decided to put me through my first "guilt test". We were in the apartment, and I was in the kitchen preparing dinner. She was mouthing off for some reason at her brother and then started in on me. I realized instantly that I didn't want to get mad at her for fear that she would be upset with me. However, the tirade only escalated when I didn't respond. Finally, and I was really struggling with this, I told her to go to her room and not to come out until she was able to speak to me and her brother with more respect. She immediately stomped off to her room and slammed the door.

When dinner was ready, I went to her room and asked her if she was ready to sit with us. She said yes and apologized to both of us. We had a great evening and she seemed much happier after this incident. I wondered for a long while after whether she had been testing me that night. Maybe she was trying to find out how far she could go. I wondered if she wanted me to assert a limit like I would have done prior to the separation. It has crossed my mind on more than one occasion that if I hadn't taken a firm stand with her on that night, I might have lost my ability to discipline her altogether.

The Divide and Conquer Test

My son's guilt tests were not quite as subtle as my daughter's outburst. As a matter of fact he attempted to be quite the opportunist. He quickly learned that the "guilt" factor could have material benefits for him. If he thought I would say "no" to something, he would quickly answer that "Mommy lets me do this, buy that, watch that television show." I believe he felt he could take advantage of a possible communication breakdown between his mother and me. I felt I was in tune to the game he was playing although occasionally he got his way simply because I would have given in before the separation. Fortunately, his mother and I were fairly consistent when dealing with him, so it was easy to verify his statements.

A Hug and a Kiss

Too much explaining can be too much for the children. A hug and a kiss can say much more than any words will. The good thing is that most children will accept them regardless of age. Of course you have to be a little more discrete as they get older. You wouldn't want to embarrass them in front of their friends!

It is important to provide your children with affection, and physical contact is crucial. Chances are it will make you feel better too! They grow up quickly, so while they are young is a good time to demonstrate your true feelings for them. The closeness that you provide can give them a security blanket that goes well beyond the walls of your home.

About Parenting Together

If the parenting skills that you use are similar to those of your former wife, then you are in an advantageous situation. Remember not to cast judgment on decisions she might make with the children. As long as the children are not put in danger, she has a right to make her own decisions. If you are able to, consult with her on any issue that you think will arise. The children will appreciate the fact that the two of you are communicating in a positive manner.

I've worked with children who act up as a means to bring their parents together because it is the only time they communicate. My former wife and I always discuss birthday and Christmas presents to avoid duplication. We've never bothered to try and "out-buy" each other when buying presents for the children. If you start doing that, you are right back into playing into the "guilt" hand.

"Why don't you love Mommy anymore?"

My son was very direct in his approach. One particular guilt test stands out. It is probably a situation that many dads have faced. It happened one day when my son and daughter and I were driving in the car. Out of the blue he asked, "Why don't you love Mommy anymore?" I sometimes wonder if he knew he had a captive audience in the car that day when asking that question. I probably should have seen this type of question coming from him and yet, on some level, I probably did anticipate it. I found myself sucking back air and then spoke as both children listened intently. I kept the answer simple and said, "I do love Mommy, Zach. Daddy just isn't in love with Mommy anymore." There was a brief moment of silence in the car and then they moved the conversation to another topic.

The incident passed as quickly as it had arrived. I'm still not sure whether that was a good answer or not, but it was the best I could do with short notice. When answering children it is important to be sensitive to what they are going through as well. They are not interested in hearing their father put down their mother.

Listen to Your Children

A few years later my daughter announced that a friend was going to live with one of her parents following their divorce because the other parent did not love her. It was a good opportunity to explain why children live with a particular parent more often than their other parent. I made sure it was clear that love was not usually an issue at all. I explained to her that I wanted her and her brother to live with me, but that I also wanted them to have the opportunity to live in the home where they had grown up. I felt that this was an opportunity to give my daughter some insight into the situation. I believe it is important to listen and clarify misunderstandings as the children get older, particularly if it does not seem to be hurting anyone.

It will be difficult to pass these "guilt" tests and other issues if you continue to be frustrated, angry, depressed, or disillusioned. Of course it doesn't mean that you won't have some of these feelings at times. You will, but they can't dominate your life. If they do, you will become a dysfunctional dad and your children will not want to spend time with you. You will see less and less of them and everyone will suffer.

16. Healthy Distractions

When newly separated I believe it is important to have some healthy distractions that will help give you a new direction in your life. Refinishing furniture and decorating helped me get back on my feet. This chapter will look at some of the other activities that helped me, but it is important to find those things that are of interest to you personally.

Cooking

Cooking is something you can do in your own place. It is very therapeutic and it reinforces a healthy lifestyle. Besides, if you eat healthier, there is a better chance that you will be around longer for your children. There is no extra expense to this activity and it is a lot cheaper than eating out every night. If your comfort level with eating alone at home is not high and you like to be out with your friends, then you can quickly get into eating out every night. It can get quite costly. An alternative is to have pot-lucks at your new home.

You will need a basic cookbook like *The Joy of Cooking*, regardless of whether or not you are planning to become a master chef. People often have a lot of cookbooks. Maybe someone will give you one, or you can find one in a garage sale. If you don't have pots, find a kitchen store and wait for a sale. I bought good quality pots one at a time as they went on sale. They happened to have small factory defects, so they were a lot cheaper. It is definitely worth it to buy top quality cooking utensils. They work better and they will last forever. At first you should try simple recipes, and you never know, you might learn to enjoy it.

I quickly learned that my children were not interested in going out to eat when they were with me. I believe that they took comfort in seeing me working in the kitchen and smelling their dinner on the stove. Whenever they came over, I made a point of having sit-down meals with them. There was no television allowed when we were eating dinner. It helped me keep in touch with what was going on in their lives. They shared stories with me and I learned what had happened in school, who their friends were, and what music they were listening to at the time. I didn't plan that my new interest in cooking would have so many positive side effects, but I'm glad it did.

Involve the Children
I would often try and make the meal something they could get involved with too. For instance, they loved it when we made pizza. I would make a point of going to the grocery store with them so they could choose the toppings. At home, they would help with the preparations. We'll often still do this today. My son, now fourteen, surprised me with an amazing Caesar salad the other night, so I guess he has learned something about cooking as well.

Mealtime is Family Time
The reason I have spent a fair amount of time on this particular interest is because the time in the kitchen and

mealtime represented a normalcy that we all needed following the separation. It felt good to be in each other's company without the "separation cloud" lingering over our heads. These moments continue to be the bright spots for us during rough times in our lives.

Structure

Children need structure and fathers who are setting up a new home need to incorporate structure into the new environment. Fathers need to create routines that are consistent. Fathers are not babysitters. A father is not there simply to fill in when mom has to go out. Fathers have to be careful about falling into that trap. A father is a primary caregiver and fathers should not become secondary in their children's lives. I never saw my own father as often as I saw my mother but I never considered him as a secondary influence in my life.

Fathers have to do more than find a place to live. They need to establish a caring home for their children. That home will be a place where caring is a given, respect is expected, and routines are followed. Children will quickly recognize that they still have their dad even though he lives in a different home.

Hiking

I got into hiking a few years prior to my separation. It is a wonderful way to be outdoors, get exercise, and not spend a lot of money. Following the separation I did a few hikes, and I felt it was a wonderful change of pace. It was so nice to go out and have some fun and not have to worry about all the details of getting my life in order. In addition, I was with some good friends who were very supportive. Activities such as this can help a father become healthier, happier, and stronger following the trauma of a separation.

The key for any father is to find the activity that will make him feel better. Some people prefer team sports. For instance, joining a softball team can give you similar feelings and is also very inexpensive. Over the years, I have participated in both team and individual sports and find that I happen to prefer individual sports. That does not mean that I do these sports alone. However, my success or failure in these activities is dependent on my own abilities and I like that aspect of it. In many ways, getting to know his limitations and strengths helps a father understand himself and be a better father.

Walking

Healing was helped by the long walks that I took almost daily. I had moved to a great neighborhood so I decided to take advantage of it. Sometimes I'd go for walks late at night and other times I'd go early in the morning. At times, I went to exercise my body, and at other times I went to clear my mind. This simple and most cost–effective activity helped me clear my head so that I could plan a new direction for myself. That could be as simple as planning what to do the next day or as complicated a sorting out my financial situation. Working through all this during the walks left time to enjoy my children without distractions when they were over. Sometimes we would go out for walks together and I would bring a camera. We would look at the ducks down by the lake or walk around an old house that they thought was haunted. They're fond memories for me.

Bicycling

That twenty-five dollar bicycle came in handy. I used it to build up my cardiovascular fitness. It became quite the challenge to see how far I could bike on early summer mornings. The ride made me feel great and I loved the cool shower afterwards. It released all the tension in my body that had been built up during the separation. The children seemed to like the idea that I was taking care of myself. I believe it showed them that their father was going to be okay. Obviously life was different for all of us, but there was a feeling that we were going to make it. And the important thing was that we were taking a healthy approach to solving some of our problems. I had no interest in hanging out in bars talking to other divorced dads. I wanted to continue being a father first. Meeting women at singles dances was not a priority for me. I wanted to feel good about myself again and be there for my two children.

Music

Music helped me. Music has a way of shaping your mood and soothing your mind. I've loved it all my life and although I don't play an instrument, I have an extensive CD collection. In the early years following the separation, those CDs helped me through a lot of emotional highs and lows. It helped me get my life back in order.

My children share this love of music and we definitely used this common interest to stay close. They introduced me to some of the music they were listening to on the radio and I shared some of the music that I was listening to when I was their age. We continue to do this today and I don't ever see this activity ending.

17. Being Alone versus Being Lonely

All the activities mentioned in the last chapter helped me get through probably the toughest period in my life. There are many other healthy activities that fathers can think of to help themselves. A dad has to find out what he enjoys and what actually makes him feel better. There is a big difference between being alone and being lonely. It is okay to be alone if you are comfortable with yourself. It is not okay if you are unhappy and don't feel like a whole person without someone at your side.

I am quite comfortable living alone now. I have done it for a number of years. Any divorced father who can't shake the feeling of being lonely should seek professional help. There is no shame in admitting that you are having difficulty adjusting to the changes that have occurred in your life.

If you are sad because of the separation it is important to put on a brave face for the children. They have been traumatized too. The children will not want to see their dad breaking down every weekend because he is so sad. Just because a father may be hurting doesn't mean that he has to take it out on the children. It is okay to share with the children that you are hurting by explaining how you are feeling. However, it is important to tell them that things will get better.

It is not fair to take out your frustrations on them. They need their father to support and help them at this time. This makes it important to keep a "stiff upper lip" when the children are home with you.

Unrealistic Demands

Snapping at the children and ordering them around will only alienate them from you. Think about sharing your opinion on certain issues as opposed to telling them what to do. Imposing rules that can't be enforced only serves to weaken your authority.

When I was a young boy, I remember bringing home a friend of questionable character. My Dad came home from work early and spoke to that particular boy. I knew that would be a problem. However, my Dad was smart. He knew he wasn't home all day and couldn't control my friends or me. At the dinner table that night he simply said, "You know, I don't really like you hanging out with that boy." The message was received loud and clear. I knew my father was right. Of course, I never told him as much. The point is that you can't control everything. You have to have faith in your child's ability to make the right decisions. They will always need your guidance and modeling. As fathers we should always be paying attention to our children's lives. Ultimately, they will have to have the tools to make their own life decisions. The guidance that fathers provide eventually helps them make better decisions.

Getting Professional Help

A family doctor can recommend someone to help if

necessary. Many communities have social service agencies that can also provide assistance. Divorced fathers' groups are also available in larger cities. If you are a member of a church organization, then very often they can put you in contact with someone. Professionals can have problem solutions that you may never have considered. You owe it to yourself and your children to seek help.

Be Patient with the Children

The children need to have time to adjust as well. It is important to keep a close eye on how they are coping. They have to be given time to become accustomed to their new life. They continue to need the love and understanding that a father can give. The strategies you use will shape your relationship with them for years to come. I made a number of choices in order to remain an integral part of their lives.

18. Creating a New Family Dynamic

Phone Calls to Mom

One of the first things that a father will have to tolerate is the fact that the children will miss their mother when they are with him. They will probably want to telephone her. Separation anxiety is very normal under these circumstances. My children were calling their mother every hour and a half in the first few months. It was important for me to swallow my pride and accept it.

Minimize Interference

I decided to not interfere when the children wanted to call their mother. It only became a problem if they were questioning a parental decision I had made and they decided to try and get her sympathy. Fortunately, she and I had already agreed not to get involved in decisions made in each other's homes.

The phone calling can get frustrating and you do have to be secure in your role as father, particularly when you see them calling their mother frequently. They have to know that you are the parent responsible in your home. If the situation persists, you may want to talk it over with their mother, so that she doesn't always respond. Maybe the children could be told that their mother needs some quiet time.

Avoid Petty Rules

One divorced dad I know refuses to let his daughter call her mother when she is with him. In addition, he has told the mother not to phone to see how things are going with her daughter. This is insecurity and behavior like this raises everyone's anxiety level. Children like to know where their parents are and it is natural for them to want to keep in contact. The little girl in this story insists on calling her mother anyway.

As the children get used to the new apartment, they no longer feel the need to be calling their mother quite as often. However, a lot may depend on the direction that their mother's life takes. If they see her becoming more comfortable with the routine then they will too. You must be patient with yourself, your children, and maybe even your former wife. You are all not going to reach a comfort level with your new lives at the same time, so you have to allow everyone the time they need.

Dealing with Rejection

It is important that a father not take it personally when he hears one of his children state, "I don't want to come to your place anymore, Daddy!" If it is a different place than their original home then it is still strange to the children. The anxiety may even be stronger if they continue to share the original family home with their mother. They may simply be testing or they may be stating that they are more comfortable in the home they have spent more time in over the years and where they have the most "stuff".

Quality Time Together

This early period following the separation is an important time to spend with the children. I rented videos for them, but we watched them together. I didn't just sit them in front of the television and then do something else. We played cards during this time too. We had a dartboard that we enjoyed and we had chess tournaments. We also spent time listening to new CDs that we bought together. I made sure that I tucked them in and kissed them good night. My son always wanted me to sit on the side of his bed and talk to him before he went to sleep.

Mom's Support

Regardless, there remained an anxiety about the new place. This was not to be confused with what I was doing as their father. It was important for me to relay that message to their mother. I realized that I would need her support in getting them there consistently. I believe that if a mother gives in to the child and doesn't allow the child to come over, then she is giving in to the anxiety. A child will be even more reluctant to visit Dad's place if they perceive that they have their mother's approval to avoid coming. A father must ask their mother to understand that he is aware of the anxiety and is there to help them through it.

Maintaining Access

A father must be persistent in getting access to his children. I believe that things get so complicated for fathers that many of us just give up. Our society has to get beyond the misconception that if you pay your child support then everything will be alright. Everything will not be alright! Children need their fathers in their lives. Fathers cannot take a back seat in parenting and expect their children to come through this unscathed.

If you are having difficulty seeing your children on a regular basis, you must work to get them into your life. The best way to start doing this is by being a positive role model for them. Talk to their mother to try and get her to see how you feel. Failing that, try to get a third party to intervene on your behalf. Actually, that may be the preferred approach to the problem. Keep a journal and document your attempts to spend time with your children. This could help should you have to seek legal counsel in the future.

Toys and Other "Stuff"

That "stuff" that I referred to earlier is things like toys that the children have accumulated over the years. These toys will obviously change as they get older. However, they will certainly want some of these things around them in your place to make them feel more comfortable. I didn't try to force the issue and demand that they bring some of their toys over. I let it happen naturally so that each time they came, they brought something else and usually left it in their bedroom.

Originally they brought stuffed animals to place on their beds. Slowly Paddington Bear and assorted Beanie Babies began to appear. Even though my children are teenagers now, the stuffed animals are still there. Some of the other toys have changed to Walkmans and other gadgets. But it all means the same thing: they feel that much more comfortable calling my place their home too. Anxiety about going from one home to the other is no longer an issue.

Friendships

A father also has to understand that, at a certain age, the children will want to spend more time with their friends. It is important to be comfortable with this, so that they feel they can bring their friends over to your place. It helps to get the phone numbers of your children's friends. This way if you want them to play together, you will be able to contact that child's parents. That is another reason why copying that old directory makes things easier. However, if you know the street and your child has the number memorized, you will have easy access to the home. Contact with friends while at your home also represents continuity for the children and makes staying at your place seem like a natural thing to be doing.

When the children were younger I made a point of taking them to their friends or having their friends over to the apartment. This also allowed their friends to have a frame of reference when my kids spoke about their Dad's place. It was not some strange place far away but somewhere they had been, and it gave my children more comfort when discussing it with them.

As the children grew older, I arranged for sleepovers. This was great for me because I was able to get to know their friends as well as observe the interaction. It was not the most comfortable in a small apartment, but it was well worth it. Some of those teenagers have come up to me years later and remarked how they enjoyed the French toast I made them in the morning.

I know of a father who told his little boy that he didn't want his friends to come over. I'm not sure what the logic was. Maybe the father wanted to spend his time solely with his son. However, sooner or later peers become very important to them. If this father doesn't change his position, his son won't want to come over anymore.

As my children have grown older I have seen how important their friends are to them. Where once Mommy and Daddy were the center of their lives, friends become much more influential. This is quite normal in teenagers and a father would be wise to be very aware of who his child's friends are so when your children mention them you can carry on a conversation with them. Friendships can be trying at times and as a father you will have to be there to support your children through the ups and downs. It is important to be patient as well as a good listener.

Your Friends Too!

Don't forget to invite some of those old "couple" friends over that you would have spent time with when you were married. This helps with the transition and chances are they have children who are friends with yours. I made a point, right after the separation, of inviting people for dinner whom my children knew. The children seemed to like seeing me entertain in this manner. I believe it meant things were getting back to normal even though life would be different.

It is important that the children see their father having a good time with friends. However, they don't want him to turn into a party animal. They want to see that you are okay, so they will feel safe. They will not feel safe if the party life is a priority and it is combined with heavy drinking. The key is to remember that you are trying to bring more stability to their lives.

As time went by, I slowly introduced the children to new friends who came into my life. In your new surroundings and possibly different lifestyle you may meet people who have similar interests. A divorced father can continue to see some of the old friends but at times you can be left out of the loop.

Depending on how you or the friends feel, it may not be comfortable socializing with them. I made a point of maintaining contact but that closeness was no longer always there. However, I believe it was important for my children to see that I had friends and a life. I made a point of doing activities with these friends and the children so that they could see I was not always alone. Occasionally, I got the feeling that they worried about me living all alone.

Volunteering

Volunteering in activities that your children are involved in can really help you get back on your feet as well as foster positive rapport. This activity also goes beyond the boundaries of the custody agreement since you will be volunteering at times when the children are not at your home. This is great for everyone because it gives a father greater access. For instance, when I coached my son's baseball team for years I was able to see him and my daughter an extra two to three times per week. My daughter would often be the scorekeeper for the team.

I look back on the time I spent volunteering with fond memories. It was a good distraction from work and the stress of the separation. Working with children has a way of lifting your spirits. It was a challenge, but it was great fun. It is a great way to remain visible as a father in your community and to be a role model for your children. It gives a father a first-hand look at how his child interacts with others.

Deal with Setbacks

A father must be prepared for some setbacks during these activities as well. For instance, it took a long time for the local baseball league to figure out that a divorced father was volunteering. In the first few years they always sent written information to my former wife's home. Even phone calls for me from the league continued to go to the wrong number. It took a while for the volunteers to accept the fact that I had a separate home.

Unfortunately, many organizations are geared to work with only one home, and I believe that is one of the major reasons why fathers get left out of many important things in their children's lives. They simply do not get the information from the source because they have been displaced from their home. A lot of time and effort is spent getting their lives back on track and they miss out on important parts of their children's activities.

Vacations

I've always thought that some of the fondest memories that I have of my father come from our summer vacations.

Whether we were swimming at the beach or fishing in a rickety old rowboat, the memories are still pretty vivid and special to me. I decided soon after the separation that I would try and provide my children with a vacation each summer. This is a great way to spend time with your children in a different setting that often generates memories that they won't forget.

A vacation can be a difficult thing to do without money. I got lucky that first summer and was able to take some short trips. Some friends invited the children and me to their cottage for three days. We had a great time together and my children still talk about that trip. I believe it was another way for them to see that things were getting better. I managed to get a cottage for one week in the mountains near where I live. I did this by tutoring a student during the summer in exchange for a week at his parent's cottage. It worked out great for everyone and was a cheap vacation for us.

The children were able to play at the beach and in the woods each day, and we were only a short drive from home. We have continued to have brief vacations every year since that first summer. I'm glad I decided to do it because my children are quickly approaching the age when they will have summer jobs and won't be able to go away with me anymore.

When planning a vacation, remember that you don't have to make it elaborate. You can stay close to home. You may have ignored vacation spots that exist right in your own backyard that are not costly. We have spent many a day sightseeing right in our own city. These excursions can provide lasting memories for children. If you have little time off, make a point of setting aside three or four days to do something special with the children. A father will never get the time back, so take advantage of it. You're giving the children a memory that will last them forever.

Special Holidays and Events

Holidays and special events can be difficult for divorced families to maneuver around. It is important that time to be spent with the children for special events be worked out well in advance to avoid major battles. You and your former wife will be doing the children a big favor by ironing these out ahead of time. There are two rules that I always tried to follow. The first was that the children and I would always have a celebration together for a special event. The second rule was that I would always try and involve relatives. A divorced father needs to establish traditions for him and the children together.

It is important not to piggy-back on someone's celebration such as their mother's or a grandparent's. The traditions a divorced father establishes early on will remain with the children. Those traditions will be things they come to enjoy and will look forward to.

Christmas

Christmas was an easy holiday for us to organize because my family celebrated Christmas Eve and my former wife's family celebrated on Christmas Day. The children were always able to be a part of my family's celebration and look forward to it each year. However, it was some of the smaller things we did that made anticipation for that holiday more special, particularly in the first year.

The first Christmas alone can be very tough and it certainly was for me. I'm sure this applies to any prominent holiday of any belief or culture. It took a lot of personal strength to get through being alone during this important time. However, I did do my best to make it meaningful for the children. I had little money, so a friend gave me an artificial Christmas tree. I managed to put some money together to buy decorations and I made a point of bringing the children with me to pick some of them out. I didn't put the tree up until the children came over and we decorated it together. With the hot chocolate and the Christmas music playing, it was a special time for the three of us.

The children knew that I baked at Christmas time because that had been a tradition for many years. I knew they would be looking for tourtière and mincemeat tarts, so I made sure I baked these when they were with me. This allowed them to appreciate those holiday baking smells just as they had in the past. My daughter made some squares from a recipe her mother had given her. We each picked out a Christmas mug at the dollar store that we would use during the holiday season. This was a difficult time for all of us, but we managed to get through it with some fond memories.

Gifts Aren't Everything!

As a child growing up with six brothers and sisters, in my family the emphasis had always been on the spirit of Christmas as opposed to getting a lot of presents. I'm not sure what presents I gave the children that year and I doubt they remember either. However, three years later when we were decorating the tree for the last time in that apartment my daughter remarked, "This place always reminds me of Christmas." Once I heard that, I assumed I must have done something right in previous years.

Keep Occupied

When the children aren't around, the reality of this type of holiday for a father can be traumatic and lonely. Here are some of the things I did to try and feel better:

▷ Spend as much time as you can with your children.
▷ Don't get sentimental and put yourself further into debt buying presents.
▷ Spend as much time as you can with friends and family.
▷ Buy a book or a magazine to read for when you are alone.
▷ Put a little something under the tree for yourself. You deserve it!
▷ Go and see a movie. Preferably a comedy.

New Year's

New Year's Eve never was a big celebration prior to the divorce so I wasn't too concerned about that holiday. As it has turned out, I've always had the children either New Year's Eve or New Year's Day. Whenever I've had them, we usually just stayed home and I would make a special dinner for us.

Regardless of the religious holidays you celebrate, it is

important that your children are included. The traditions they grow up with will come from some of the things you did together. The children will stay connected to your family and that is important. You will have to negotiate the days that the children are with you. Handled carefully, these holidays can be memorable for everyone.

Birthdays

Children's birthdays are usually very exciting for them. I've always tried to celebrate my son's and daughter's birthdays in a special way. I've done this by usually inviting family and friends over and having a special dinner, a cake, and of course they get a birthday present. I've never given a birthday party and invited their friends because that is something their mother has usually done.

19. Communicating with the Children

Planning
When the children are younger it is easier to organize and plan their time with you. As they get older it is better to examine all the options before you make any plans. Activities with friends begin to monopolize their time. It is important that you share specific plans with them and let them know that you would like them to be participants. Do this prior to them coming over, so it is clear from the start. This way they have the opportunity to rearrange plans if necessary.

Consultation is a wise route to take, particularly with teenagers who may be making their own plans. A little communication can go a long way to alleviate tension and aggravation if schedules conflict. A father needs to concentrate on maximizing the positive times during the period he has his children. You can't do that if you are constantly in conflict.

The Children Are not Messengers
A major mistake a father can make is to use the children to communicate messages to their mother. If you have been doing this, then it is time you began speaking to her directly. When differences or conflicts linger, it is best to use direct communication. It is not necessary nor is it healthy to expose

children to constant conflict between their parents. This is a situation that you can do something about. Why raise the anxiety of the children by including them in your battles? If their mother is guilty of doing this, then speak to her and tell her that you would appreciate it if she spoke to you directly and not through the children.

Make Yourself Available

How available are you to your children when they are not with you? One weekend my daughter complained that she could not reach me when she wanted to talk to me. She said that I never called her and her brother. However, they have a computer hook-up at their mother's home that prevents calls from getting through. I've called frequently, but there is no way to leave a message. She had interpreted this incorrectly as a lack of caring on my part. To solve the problem, I agreed to get a cell phone so that they could reach me at all times. This eased some of her anxiety and I am able to give them the phone when they go out so I can keep in touch with them.

Dealing with Dating

You are likely to start dating at some point following the separation. This is an area you have to approach with extreme caution as far as your children's awareness is concerned. If you suddenly add another person into the mix, it might upset everything you have accomplished to that point. I'm not advising to avoid dating, but precautions should be taken that will help you in the long run:

▷Go slowly when you meet a woman.

▷Don't introduce the woman to your children for a long while.

▷Go through the "trial and error" dating game on your own and on your own time.

▷Don't burden your children with the "up and downs" of your love life.

A child's greatest fear following a divorce is probably that of abandonment. You must be careful not to displace your children for the affection of a woman. A father does not have the luxury of spending all his time with a woman he may be in love with. The children will still need their father. If this new lady really cares, she will understand your need to spend time with your children.

A divorced dad I know once said to a friend, "If my penis was my brain, I'd be a millionaire!" This father recognized very late in life the frequency with which he had made many poor choices with women. Unfortunately, he had alienated his older children for a while as well. He is now in the process of re-establishing contact with them. It is never too late, but valuable time can never be given back.

Dating can be an exciting time, but you have to keep in mind that you have children. If you eventually become serious about someone, mention her to your children. When you want to introduce her to your children, make it for short time periods, and you can do this several times. Later you can take the plunge and invite her to an activity that includes everyone for a longer period of time. Another great way to include her is to have other friends around. This can alleviate pressure all around.

Choose Your Words Carefully

The summer I had an infection that took a long while to diagnose, I was quite miserable. My daughter got frustrated with seeing me lying around and started to get on my case. In my misery, I made the mistake of saying, "You sound just like your mother!" As soon as it came out of my mouth I knew I had made a mistake. I apologized to her later, but those words hurt her deeply. Time heals and I believe the fact that she knows I love her very much helped us get through that crisis.

Words can cut deep. Each time you interact with your children it is important to think about what you are saying. It is difficult to take something back once it has been spoken. When emotions are running high it is important to reflect before you speak.

Values

Values are something that children pick up from their parents. A father can't always be there to censor what they see or hear on television, the radio, or Internet. However, a father can certainly make them aware of what he believes is acceptable. You cannot afford to avoid putting limits on things like language and behavior. Children need to know the limits. I believe they feel safer and more comfortable when these are made clear. Unlimited access to whatever they please will only serve to distance your children from you. They will get lost in a world that you are not familiar with and probably wouldn't approve of. You could lose control over them in your own house. They need to understand the guidelines when they are young if you hope to keep them in your life as they get older.

Cleaning House

When you live alone, you get used to your home being a certain way. I like to put things in order and avoid clutter. However, when the kids come over, everything changes. Early on I had to decide whether I wanted to spend the weekends with them constantly nagging them to clean up. Like most kids, they had their toys all over and seemed to enjoy leaving a mess in the kitchen. This was quite a contrast to the look of the place when I was alone.

Compromise

We worked it out over the years through compromise. They agreed to keep the living room clean because that is a place that we all use. They now work at putting things away in the kitchen after they have raided the refrigerator. I leave their rooms to them, but they are expected to put them in order prior to leaving.

I felt it was important not to spend too much of the time I had with them disciplining them about picking up after themselves. A father would be wise not to spend time nagging at the children when he has them. After all, they are still kids! They do like to play and sometimes "mess" can be a healthy thing. They will not be able to keep things in the order you do. Just to recap, I used the following guidelines to help me:

▷ Remembered that they are children.
▷ Children like to play.
▷ Play can make a mess.
▷ Mess is okay sometimes.

▷ We are all responsible for our own mess.

▷ Certain family areas need to remain free from mess.

▷ Rooms need to be cleaned before they leave.

▷ If guests are coming over, then we all help to prepare the house.

20. Your Children and School

The School System

Staying in contact with your child's school is probably the single most important way that a father can monitor and maintain contact with his children. However, most schools are part of a rigid system that only recognizes single-home families. A father can find himself out of the information loop very quickly. There are some things you can do to keep yourself involved.

The Reaction May not Be All Positive

I've been a teacher for years yet I was still not prepared for the reaction I got when I went to my first "Meet the Teacher" night. The teacher, who knew me, never even made eye contact with me, let alone talked to me. I made the assumption because she knew both my former wife and me that she had made her own personal judgment on the separation. This was a good wake-up call for me. The school system is an old one, and there remains a stigma about divorce in general and fathers in particular. For the education system, divorce usually signals troubled children with fathers who may or may not support them and who may have minimal involvement.

Demand Notices/Reports

As a father, I found that information concerning events at

school did not always get to me in time. Sometimes I never saw them at all. Part of the difficulty was not seeing the children every day, so I wasn't there to go through their school bag each night. Sometimes information was not shared with me for reasons unknown and other times I found out about the event at the last minute. Regardless, I had to find strategies to improve the information between my home and the school.

School Calendar

The school calendar is an excellent reference for the whole school year. Most schools make these and send them to the homes of their students. Phone the school and get one sent to your home. As soon as you get it, stick it on the fridge. Each time you see your children you can use the calendar to discuss upcoming events at the school. It also shows the children that you take an interest in their schoolwork.

Other Parents

You may know parents of some of the children in your son's or daughter's class. Make sure you have some of their phone numbers. You can also ask them if they could keep you informed of any special events. Some of them may be more than happy to keep you informed about any school or class activity. I used this source quite often when my children were in elementary school.

The School Secretary

The secretary of the school is usually the pulse of the building. The principal depends on her to keep everything going.

She can be a great help in keeping track of events in the school. Call her and explain your situation and chances are she will be more than willing to help out. You don't want to be constantly calling her because she will not appreciate it. However, she does have access to files, teacher mailboxes, the principal, and a fax machine. She can handle any task or form of communication you need. She'll be even more willing to help if she feels you are a genuinely concerned parent so stay on her good side!

Teacher Names

Know the names of your child's teachers. Your child will be spending five days a week with these people. They are qualified people who will know your child's academic standing, work habits, and social and emotional state. A father needs to access that information by talking and listening to these teachers. Any plan of activity you decide to make after meeting with the teachers should be discussed with your former wife. After all, you are not really a single parent, you are a divorced father who has the opportunity to monitor your child's progress with your former wife.

Involvement Should Be Timely

You don't want to be phoning teachers every week. Make calls timely and meaningful. Thank them for their time, give them your phone number, and let them know that you want to be informed should there be any issues that arise. Teachers deal with all kinds of parents, but they usually appreciate supportive parents. Your child has a greater chance of success if you work in a cooperative way with them. Maintain a relationship that is based on respect so that your children transfer those values as well.

Dealing with Issues

One issue that I had to intervene in took place when my daughter was in grade ten. She was doing very poorly in her math course all year. Early in the year, I got a math tutor for her. However, this was not successful and she failed the course. The School Board was offering a week–long tutorial in the summer prior to a supplemental exam. I decided to call Meghan's mother and suggest that she enroll in the tutorial. Fortunately, my former wife and I have seldom disagreed on appropriate courses of action to take regarding or involving our children's education. I also hired a grade eleven student to tutor her each day. My daughter did four hours of math per day for one week. She ended up getting 74 percent on the supplemental exam.

I believed that my daughter had the ability to pass this math course. I felt she had put more emphasis on her other courses and let the math marks slide. She was discouraged in class all year with her lack of success. After she got her summer results, she was thankful she had worked that hard for the week. I was glad I had been persistent about her taking the math supplemental and she felt better about her math ability.

Report Cards

It is very important to be aware of when report cards come out. This is an ideal opportunity to praise your child for something that they have accomplished. If you see areas of concern, ask for reasons why this has happened and discuss suggestions for improvement. This is a good time to offer advice and suggest strategies for them to use at school and for homework. Ask your son or daughter to come up with suggestions or strategies as well.

Positive Involvement

Whether your child's report card meets expectations or not the follow-up discussion should be positive. If deserved, a child needs to hear a father's praise. Your son or daughter has to know that you will be there to support their efforts even though results may not meet expectations all the time. Children get resistant to too much interference as they get older, so this is something that a father must monitor carefully. If your child is resisting your help, maybe you can arrange for someone else to help out on a regular basis.

The report card is an opportunity to monitor your child's progress at school. A father's comment to his child can make a tremendous difference. Stating, "I'm proud of you." shows how you feel, and saying "You must be proud of yourself" indicates that you are proud while also implying that they are really doing well for themselves. This fosters a "love of learning" message that is important for parents to give their children.

The Parent/Teacher Interview

I only remember missing one report card and subsequently one interview. I made the wrong assumption that my son's mother would keep me informed, but I realize now that it was not her responsibility to do that. Fortunately, a parent of one of his classmates let me know before it was too late. I immediately called the school secretary who faxed me the report. I was not satisfied with the results so I called the teacher for an interview. Unfortunately, the teachers had to meet twice because they had already met with my former wife. At the interview we mapped out a plan for my son that we would follow up on during another interview in six weeks' time. That interview would include my son's mother.

I informed my former wife of the interview, the plan developed, and we had the follow-up meeting. She was happy that I was involved and we both worked at helping our son. He began to show signs of improvement and our follow-up meeting was very positive.

Although it may be difficult at times, try to work with your former wife to decide how to help your children get through school. Any differences of opinion should be discussed in private so as to work out a plan. Once you come up with a common strategy then try to work with the school and the child. If you can be consistent in this approach, your child's chances of success will greatly improve.

Other School Activities

Various forms of Parent/Teacher Associations meet on a regular basis at all schools. This is a great way to stay involved at the school. They usually meet just once per month, so it is not too time–consuming. It also places you in a position to access any information you might need. This could be one of those "volunteer" activities I wrote about earlier.

A child's most memorable school events usually take place outside the classroom. The football game, school play, and band concerts are only a few examples of the many special events that take place in school all year long. A father needs to be involved in the celebration of these special moments. Children will always be looking for their parents in the audience. Even if your child is not in the event, it could be a fun activity for all of you to do together. I've taken my children to plays and other events at the school only because I knew they would enjoy them.

Children Recognize the Involvement

Children will be much happier at school if their father is involved in a positive way. A father needs to have access to information. This is something he will have to initiate. He needs to communicate on a regular basis with the school. Finally, he needs to celebrate the accomplishments of his children both in and outside the classroom.

21. Family Crisis, Moving, and Extended Family

Sooner or later an event will take place that will place you in a situation that you never could have anticipated. This happened to me when my former wife called to say that a close family member had died. I was working in the same school that my daughter attended at that time, so she asked me to go and get her as she was coming to pick her up. I found my daughter with a group of friends and she immediately knew that something was wrong. I told her the news and gave her a hug. I let her friends console her until she had to leave.

While my wife was with family members, I had the children and I made a point of discussing their aunt who had just died. They were very aware that I had known her from the time I was a teenager. I shared some stories about her with them. While we were talking, my daughter said, "Why don't we go to the funeral, Dad?" I had already decided to do just that. It was ninety miles away and their mother was already there, so I was able to drive up with the children. In many ways, I think this was a great comfort to them. They had never been to a funeral before and were nervous. I explained that it was important to give your condolences to family members and to think about what a special person their aunt was.

The reception I received from my former wife's family members was touching and honest. I had not seen these people for five years. More importantly, my children were able to see this interaction. They seemed to be watching carefully, particularly when I was greeted by various family members.

They were able to see their mother and father hug and I hoped it would reinforce the words I had told my son five years earlier. We all sat and grieved together in the church and later at a reception. An event like this is unfortunately bound to happen and it is so important that a divorced dad make the effort to demonstrate to his children that he is there for them. Some of these situations can be extremely difficult, but it will bring a father and his children closer together.

Extended Family

Divorced fathers should make a point of including their children in special extended family events such as weddings and baptisms. This way they get to know and enjoy the relatives on their father's side of the family. They need to know that they are still loved members of a larger family. Take time to discuss some of the accomplishments or positive characteristics of particular family members. Positive statements like, "You have the same sense of humor as your Uncle Bruce!" help to make connections to that extended family. They should perceive themselves as being full members of their extended family.

Moving

At some point you are probably going to consider a move

from your initial place of residence following the separation. It took me three years to work up the courage to consider this. I found a small home in a great neighborhood not too far from the children's mother's home. I knew it was time to leave the apartment. The kids were very excited to be moving into a house again. My son helped with the moving and rode in the rental truck with me. Friends came over to help.

It took three years for me to feel that I could finally take care of a house again. The challenge of gardening and home repair was now exciting to me. Prior to this, I believed that they would have felt like an extra burden I didn't need. The house turned out to be a great bargain and the real estate prices in our area were beginning to turn around. If I hadn't moved when I did, I don't think I could have ever afforded to buy a house in that area again.

If a divorced father is planning a move, there are a number of issues to consider. The following are some questions you should ask yourself prior to purchase:

▷ Will the children have enough room?

▷ Are you close to their school?

▷ Can they walk or bike to your house?

▷ Will you be just as willing to see them on a regular basis even though it may be a long drive?

▷ Will the children have access to their friends from the new home?

▷ Can you afford it?

▷ Is it close to public transportation?

The children enjoy our home and in many ways it answers their needs as well as my own. One day when we were visiting my brother at his new house about twenty minutes away, we all agreed that the house was beautiful. When I suggested jokingly that maybe we should move out there their response was very clear. "No way. We would never live here because we couldn't see our friends!"

22. Living with a Girlfriend

Having worked with many families for years as an educator, I realized the trauma that can occur when a new partner appears in Dad's life. Many fathers choose to move in with a partner quickly after a separation. This can further complicate an already delicate situation. I recommend avoiding this if you want anxiety kept to a minimum.

Feelings of Abandonment
The children probably already have feelings of abandonment because you are no longer living with them full–time. If at all possible, avoid reinforcing these feelings by bringing a stranger into their lives too soon after the separation. You probably had time to grieve about your failed marriage prior to the separation. You have had time to come to grips with that reality.

Children need that opportunity as well. It is important to respect the feelings of hurt, shock, and insecurity that they are only just beginning to come to terms with. However, if you have already taken the plunge and moved in with your girlfriend, there may still be time to salvage the situation before it goes from bad to worse.

Understand Your Own Insecurities
It is quite normal to feel insecure following a divorce and

seek the immediate comfort of another partner. I felt this way. However, I thought it was important to first get on my own two feet. My initial fear was that I was going to be alone for the rest of my life. These anxieties can leave you open to rash decisions that could prove harmful later. By living alone, I got to know more about myself. I realized that I could take care of myself, my home, my children, and get help when I needed it. Many men do end up living with someone else following a marriage breakup, yet the primary focus should always be the well–being of your children.

Respect their Feelings

Children have a variety of feelings when another woman begins sharing their father's life. They may show this by becoming very quiet or by throwing temper tantrums. It is important that a father recognize the concern and reassure the children that they remain the top priority in his life. Of course if a child is sleeping for unusually long periods of time or is endangering him or herself through self-mutilation, it is important that you seek professional help for them.

Other indicators can be their performance at school or a change in their eating habits. You continue to be their father and therefore you must look for indicators that demonstrate the emotional state of your children. Listen to them and look for changes in behavior that could require attention.

You and the Children Together

Whether you have moved in with someone or not, there are ways that you can make the transition easier on the children. If you ask yourself what you think they need, the answer will be quite simple: You! Therefore, give them more of yourself. Spend time alone with them, by bringing them to the park, taking them for walks, or simply taking the time to listen to them. They do have things they want to tell you. Let them get used to the new lady in your life over time. If you try to force her on them, they may end up resenting her before you've barely begun.

Make a point of taking the children to visit old friends with just them. This will help ease the transition. Take them out for lunch on your own and listen to what they have to say. You may want to meet with them at their school with their teachers to see how things are going.

If you coached or volunteered in any of their activities prior to the separation, this would be an ideal activity to continue. There is no harm in continuing these things even though you may be living with someone. Approach a new "live-in" relationship with extreme caution when it comes to your children's feelings.

The Girlfriend as a Friend to the Children

A girlfriend can also be sensitive to the type of contact she has with the children. Initially, if the children initiate contact with her, then it is a good sign that they are testing her based on her discussions with them. She should be careful to stick to "safe" topics, like what she thought of a movie that you rented.

A partner should avoid being a disciplinarian for a long while. She should try to foster a friendship with the children. Their relationship should grow from that level. In the end, when the children are with their father, he is the sole disciplinarian. As a result, there is less chance of the girlfriend being alienated by them. By doing this, the children are allowed more flexibility in bringing the partner into their world, as they feel more comfortable.

A father who has moved in with someone else quickly following a divorce can expect a degree of resentment from the children for an extensive period of time. One father I know had to deal with this when his son was caught skipping school. The son tried to cloud the skipping issue by blaming the father's new wife for his parent's separation. This anger had been lingering for five years in the boy.

Although this boy lived with his father all the time, he still blamed him for the divorce. The father listened to his son. They had a close relationship and there was a lot of love there. The boy never skipped high school again and is now in college. This father had recognized the hurt his son felt, but he refused to buy into a guilt trip over a marriage that had ended five years earlier. He did not involve his new wife and it was dealt with between himself and his son.

Your Value System
The harmony that you and your new partner bring to the home will have a lot to do with the value system that you both have. Will the manner in which you deal with your children be acceptable to her? One father I met was foolish enough to move into the home of a woman who didn't

want his children there. It was a very selfish act and his children were extremely resentful. I met his children a few years later and unfortunately their prospect for a happy future was not bright at all.

Protect Assets

One of the things you have to consider doing if you are thinking of moving in with someone is protecting your assets. An agreement along the lines of a prenuptial agreement will benefit you and your children should things not work out with your new partner. My attorney advised me that I should get documents signed that would guarantee "separation of property" for both individuals. In other words, what I brought into a relationship I would keep should it not work out. Obviously, laws on these things vary depending on where you live.

The best thing to do is get legal advice if you are considering sharing a home with someone. This really never changes whether you are newly separated or have been divorced for ten years. It is important to protect your interests and those of your children. If the person you are moving in with loves you, then it will make no difference to her. If there is a problem with her signing then you should reconsider the relationship.

Clarify Needs

As much as we hate to admit it, most men are dependent on women as a measure of their own self-esteem. To a large extent I guess many of us feel that our identity as a man is much clearer as long as there is a woman at our side.

However, it is important to clarify who we are, how we feel, and what we need following a divorce. This can be achieved much more easily by being alone for a while.

Children need their fathers even more following a divorce. A father would be wise to try to avoid having another relationship too quickly. The children are the people a father should care about above everything else, but they will have to see it, hear it, and most of all, feel it. A girlfriend will have to feel secure enough to accept that. It is important that fathers stay involved and remain a positive influence in their children's lives forever. After all, children only have one father and, to repeat a point I've already made, a failed marriage does not mean you have failed as a parent.

23. The Blended Family

The blended family can work, but everyone must understand their role. The Brady Bunch used to make it seem easy and romantic but it is far from that simple. In addition to looking at all the factors that I have talked about, you have to look at the whole dynamic within the other family. That dynamic is probably quite different from what you have established with your own children. It is likely that there will be a difference of opinion on many issues even before you live together. So a divorced father has to ask himself, "Are all members of both families willing to work this through together?"

This type of commitment will affect everyone for years to come. It would be wise to seek out family counselors who will walk you through many of the pitfalls that you might encounter. There is no point going into this type of commitment with your eyes closed. I have worked with many blended families over the years and the degree of success they achieve has a lot to do with the determination of both partners. There are so many dynamics going on in a blended family that it can be much more work than one's first marriage.

Don't be surprised if the children suffer an emotional setback when you announce plans to remarry. This is a wake–up call for them. They might have been holding on to an imaginary belief that you and their mother would one day get back together. They'll need a fair amount of time to adjust to the new plan. It is important that you talk to the children about this. Don't be too exuberant. It may only alienate them more.

Evaluate your role with your girlfriend's children:

> ▷ How do they perceive you?
> ▷ What role do you want to have with them?
> ▷ Will your opinion be respected?
> ▷ Are they happy and comfortable with you as their stepfather?
> ▷ Are you prepared to deal with a child who may resent your presence?
> ▷ Can you walk away and let your new wife discipline her children?

Your children will have to learn to accept their new stepmother:

> ▷ Will she be perceived as a threat to their mother's role?
> ▷ Will they accept her authority?
> ▷ Will their mother encourage cooperation?
> ▷ Will your new wife be comfortable looking after their basic needs if her affection is rejected?

Obviously, if your former wife is happy and secure, your new relationship will be non-threatening. All the adults involved need to get along if the blended family has any chance of survival. Everyone arrives at this situation with separate agendas and individual baggage, including Dad. The important thing is for all parties to recognize this beforehand so that it is easier to deal with when crises erupt.

I knew of one blended family where the stepmother actually took over control of her stepson's education. The mother and father would come to the interviews, but the stepmother would be the spokesperson. It was an interesting dynamic and each of the participants seemed comfortable with it. I was probably the most uncomfortable person in the room.

Very often the upbringing of the child remains under the domain of the natural parents. The step-parent learns to disengage in times of crisis as the parents sort things out. However, there are obviously exceptions such as the one discussed above.

The dynamic within the blended family is quite complicated. I've only touched on a few of the possibilities. As complicated as life can be living alone following a divorce, life in a blended family can become overwhelming.

Having Another Child

I decided years ago that I was not going to have another child, so it was not an issue for me. However, many divorced dads meet someone and the couple decides to have a baby together. There are obviously many factors that one has to consider before making that commitment. The biggest concern is to consider carefully how your children are going to react to a baby brother or sister. I have seen many different scenarios. Children in these situations can grow up loving and caring about each other.

If you only have your children part of the time, a new child will certainly cut into the time you are able to spend with your children. At the same time the new baby will need its father as well. This is a real test of a father's capacity to give. You need to have a fair amount of free time to give to these children. A divorced father will have to share his love with all of the children involved if they are to ever establish a sense of family. Alienation of any child can lead to a very unhappy situation for years to come.

The saddest case I ever worked on at school was a situation where the couple had married, had a baby girl, divorced, remarried, and each had babies again. By the time I met with them, their teenage daughter was having many difficulties. She had been in detention centers since she was thirteen for drug and alcohol use. She was a great kid and the parents were nice people. The problem was that both parents had become totally wrapped up in their new lives. The daughter was the odd person out and she knew it. She had been tossed back and forth like a bouncing ball while the needs of the new babies were catered to. These parents loved their daughter but they just hadn't given her the time she needed.

The blended family is a tremendous challenge that should be treated as such. As there are so many individuals involved, it cannot be entered into lightly. With a lot of love to go around, there is the possibility that the individuals will grow to care for each other as family.

A divorced father's own children must feel unthreatened. Paying too much attention to a new child in the family could be extremely upsetting to your children initially. A father doesn't want to risk alienating his own children. Even the most confident children can quickly feel that their father's affections are being given elsewhere. Continue to tell and demonstrate to your children how much you love them. Feelings of insecurity will only escalate if they are ignored.

24. In Conclusion

The Children as the Priority

In the years following the separation it is important that the children remain the priority in your life. They need to see evidence of this constantly and consistently. All of the hobbies, interests, and activities I have discussed do not occupy a great deal of my time when the children are with me. A divorced father does not want to be golfing all of one day when he only sees his son or daughter for two! It can be tempting to go to an event and leave the children with a babysitter or family member. However, as much as a child may love his grandmother or aunt, it is not really fair that he/she spend half his/her weekend with them during a father's time.

Children of divorce need involved dads. A father can't assume it is okay to go off and do something else for hours on end. As the children get older and less dependent, they will have their own friends and activities that may not include you. This will provide you with all the time you need to pursue the things that interest you. However, it is important to be patient because their timeline may not be the same as yours.

For a number of years I made a point of not going out at all when I had the children. People who knew me realized this. I figured that the kids really didn't need me picking them up on Thursday and then getting a babysitter for them on Friday. I felt this would be unfair and that eventually the children would not want to come over.

Social Life

There is no doubt that it is important to have a social life. However, if you are hanging out with friends with similar values, they will understand your need to be home with your children. There are always other opportunities to get together with friends when the children are not at your home. At some point in the future, when the children are leading healthy and productive lives, both you and your children will be grateful for the commitment.

Taking Care of Yourself

Over the years it is important for a divorced father to continue to evaluate what his needs are in life. Obviously, the children are a priority, but you have to remain focused when you are setting goals and objectives for yourself. Check out the little things around you before you begin to deal with the big picture. For instance, are you an organized person at home? If the answer is no, then attempt to change that habit.

- ▷ Put things away when you take them out.
- ▷ Don't procrastinate on tasks that need to be done.
- ▷ Make regular clean–up schedules.
- ▷ Pay bills on time.
- ▷ Have a well stocked fridge, so you are not tempted to eat out all the time.
- ▷ Organize bureaus and cupboards.

I enjoy each day by starting it off with a cup of tea. I like working, but I prefer a relaxed atmosphere at work. My children, on the other hand, are used to not having breakfast. I don't approve of this but they are used to a much more fast-paced atmosphere in the morning. I move at a different pace and even though they have never been late for school, they are constantly worried about being late. We have come to recognize that we do things differently in the morning. It is not really a question of right or wrong. It is important that you can be yourself in your own home. The children need to know that Dad has his own life too!

For divorced fathers, it is so important to maintain a sense of self-dignity. Yet dignity can easily slip away from fathers who feel their whole world is crashing down around them. It is important for a father to keep his head high and take pride in his role as a father. That means that not only does a father feel obligated but also happy to provide the necessary time and love needed to help raise his children. It requires a commitment to model behaviors and values that will enrich a child's life.

The justice system has an obligation to help fathers maintain their dignity as parents. This has everything to do with fair judgments with regard to custody and child support. The legal system needs to recognize fathers for the role they play in a child's life. If a father's dignity is stripped because of unjust custody and child–support rulings, then the child is the big loser. Fairness is what is important and it is a lot more than just the financial arrangements of a divorce. Fathers have an equal right to have access to their children.

Reflection

One of the most important things that a divorced father can do is to reflect on what you have accomplished as time goes by. It is important to see if you have made strides in improving how you feel and how your life is compared to the time around the initial separation. This means looking at those obvious accomplishments such as work performance, and material wealth, but more importantly looking inward to recognize how you feel emotionally. Do you feel happier than a year earlier? Depending on your answer, it is important to take the necessary steps to make adjustments to your life if needed.

It Is Never Too Late!

It is never too late to repair relationships with your children if you are willing to try. I remember encouraging a father and son to talk to each other. The son was sixteen and resented his father for leaving his mother. Years later the son came back to the school to talk to me and he said that he and his dad had finally decided to talk and that they were meeting for lunch. The unfortunate part was that they were both good people. For whatever reason, the son had been turned off the dad at an early age and the dad had become bitter and resentful and, as a result, withdrew from his role as a parent. For years they never spoke—yet they lived only minutes from each other.

Accept the Change

A divorced father must accept that his life has changed. That life may not be what he envisioned, but he has to be happy with it and himself. Eventually that happiness will allow his children to see the real person that is their dad. It will help them to find happiness in their own lives. As time passes, life will return to a new normalcy that will allow your children to find their own way.

This framework for divorced dads is not a magic pill that will make everything better. I hope it illustrates the hard work and commitment needed to be a good father following a divorce. Being a father is not a responsibility to be shirked. As a divorced dad, parenthood becomes more complicated.

A divorced father's children need to remain an integral part of his life. A new beginning for Dad does not exclude the children. However, it will require all the patience, love, and ingenuity that a father is able to generate. A divorced father and his children deserve to share in a happy life together.